The
RESURRECTION
of
MINISTRY

Serving in the Hope of the Risen Lord

ANDREW PURVES

An imprint of InterVarsity Press
Downers Grove, Illinois

InterVarsity Press
P.O. Box 1400, Downers Grove, IL 60515-1426
World Wide Web: www.ivpress.com
E-mail: email@ivpress.com

InterVarsity Press® is the book-publishing division of InterVarsity Christian Fellowship/USA®, a
movement of students and faculty active on campus at hundreds of universities, colleges and schools
of nursing in the United States of America, and a member movement of the International Fellowship
of Evangelical Students. For information about local and regional activities, write Public Relations
Dept., InterVarsity Christian Fellowship/USA, 6400 Schroeder Rd., P.O. Box 7895, Madison, WI
53707-7895, or visit the IVCF website at <www.intervarsity.org>.

Design: Cindy Kiple

Images: Lonny Kalfus/Getty Images

ISBN 978-0-8308-3741-0

Printed in the United States of America ∞

Library of Congress Cataloging-in-Publication Data

Purves, Andrew, 1946-
   The Resurretion of ministry: serving in the hope of the risen Lord
/Andrew Purves.
      p. cm.
   Includes bibliographical references and index.
   ISBN 978-0-8308-3741-0 (pbk.: alk. paper)
   1. Church work.   2. Pastoral theology.   3. Jesus
Christ—Resurrection.   I. Title.
   BV660.3.P87 2010
   253—dc22
2010000186

P	18	17	16	15	14	13	12	11	10	9	8	7	6	5	4	3	2	1
Y	25	24	23	22	11	19	18	17	16	15	14	13	12	11	10			

Dedicated with respect, gratitude

and affection to my friends

Bill Carl

President

Pittsburgh Theological Seminary

Barry Jackson

Academic Dean

Pittsburgh Theological Seminary

And to *Cathy*,

as always, with all my love,

gratitude and respect

CONTENTS

PREFACE

I AM VERY GRATEFUL TO THOSE ministers in the United States, Canada, South Africa and Namibia who encouraged me to get on with the writing of this book. I am grateful also for the insights, suggestions and critical comments made by those who reviewed the first draft. While a book is the responsibility of the author, others play important roles as encouragers, critics and reviewers. The outcome is most certainly a better book.

Pittsburgh Theological Seminary is a supportive community of learners and teachers, and I have benefited greatly from the affection of colleagues and encouragement from students. This book is in part the result of the generous sabbatical policy the faculty enjoy.

Scottish Reformed theologians informed some of what follows. First, I acknowledge my indebtedness to my teachers Thomas F. Torrance and James B. Torrance. Second, one book especially has had a major impact on my thinking and to some significant extent has shaped the movement of my presentation, namely, *The Resurrection of Our Lord* by William Milligan. Milligan's book was first published in 1881. He was professor of divinity and biblical criticism in the University of Aberdeen from 1860 and died in 1892. His lovely book (see also his *The Ascension and Heavenly Priesthood of Our Lord*) is a treasure of biblical theology. I heartily recommend it. It is a pious book in the very best sense. Although not referenced in my text, Milligan's book is reflected often in the pages that follow.

INTRODUCTION

Looking Beyond Faith and Ministry in the Mood of Holy Saturday

"Is the Lord among us or not?" (Exodus 17:7)

IN MY PREVIOUS BOOK *The Crucifixion of Ministry*, I used the intentionally shocking imaging that God kills our ministries when they get into the center of things. Our ministries are not redemptive; only the ministry of Jesus is redemptive. So our messianic pretensions are killed by God. In this sequel I will look at the resurrection of ministry. God raises up our ministries on their proper ground in the ministry of the resurrected and ascended Jesus, and we minister henceforth in the joy and hope of his life. Through the Holy Spirit binding us into union with Jesus, we share in both his resurrected life and his resurrected ministry.

THE MOOD OF HOLY WEEK
Fine and good. But do we believe it? The context to which I am writing is my sense that many of us are stuck in the mood of am-

biguity and powerlessness of Holy Saturday. Let me explain what
I mean.

In the congregation where I worship and where my wife is minister, there is a studied liturgical drama to the Holy Week services,
from Palm Sunday to Holy Saturday. Palm Sunday is an emotion-
ally complex experience. Set in the context of Lent, it anticipates
Easter. Yet we know that getting there involves the journey through
difficult days that follow. There is something of the feeling of a
false dawn to Palm Sunday, given that we know what lies ahead in
the commemoration of Holy Week. It is Easter "light." We wave
our palm branches as the children parade around the sanctuary.
We celebrate the remembrance of the arrival of King Jesus into
Jerusalem: "Hosanna to the Prince of Peace." Yet we sing our
praises knowing the terrible story that is soon to unfold. It is the
beginning of a week filled with deepening ambiguity. This is cap-
tured for me in the familiar words by Henry Milman (1820) that
we sing at the close of the service:

> Ride on, ride on, in majesty,
> In lowly pomp, ride on to die.

Knowing what lies ahead separates Palm Sunday from a parade
at Disney World. Rightly, Palm Sunday is also called Passion Sunday.

On Maundy Thursday the service has an increasingly somber
feel to it. Darkness is anticipated rather than experienced. The
"celebration" of the Lord's Supper seems ambiguous, for this is the
commemoration of the Last Supper on the night Jesus was betrayed. We celebrate knowing what is about to unfold. The next
day looms just off stage, waiting to begin its terrible story. The
mood of the worship is sealed at the close of the service when the
sanctuary is stripped of decorations in preparation for the follow-

ing day. The paraments covering the pulpit and Communion table are solemnly folded and carried out of the sanctuary as the congregation sings the mournful song "Go to Dark Gethsemane." There is no blessing. The service ends on, as it were, a flat note.

Good Friday is the day of crucifixion, the day of the death of Jesus. Everything about the liturgy is in a minor key. The sanctuary is bare for the service of commemoration—no banners, no paraments and no color. The only "decorations" are a small cross draped in black ribbon on the bare Communion table and a Paschal candle flickering weakly with a joyless light. Certainly it is the day for a crucifix, for Jesus is on the cross, and not for an empty cross, which is a symbol of the resurrection. The characteristic Protestant symbol of Christianity is strangely wrong on Good Friday. As the Tenebrae service progresses, and as the account of the Passion is read slowly, the church is darkened in stages, as if we are walking deeper and deeper into a tomb. The service ends with the extinction of the Paschal candle, the Christ candle, and it is removed from the sanctuary, an act filled with heavy symbolism. The darkness is complete. With his death, Christ, as it were, has left the building. There is no closing hymn, no blessing and no postlude. A quiet leaving is all that is left to do as the minister presses a blunt nail into our hands at the door of the church, a symbol of the day and its terrible events.

Holy Saturday is the day of emptiness. In Protestant congregations there are no services. In the Roman Catholic Church no masses are said. Worship is suspended! It is a day without liturgy—the work of the people in praise of God. It is a day without a Gospel reading in the daily lectionary. What do we do while Jesus lies in the cold of Joseph's tomb? The day feels like a gap, a space, a blank; it seems to have no legitimate content of its own. There is a hole in the universe. It is a day of waiting; traditionally, it is a day of fasting.

Even theology breaks down, for there is nothing yet to say. It is a day when the power of God is felt as deepest mystery in its absence. What is the Father doing? What does Jesus' descent into hell mean? Is it possible on this day to speak of the grief of God, even of the loneliness within God? Why did it take three days for Jesus to be raised from death? The danger of crude anthropomorphizing is obvious, and our language stretches to the limits of reference. What are we to make of Holy Saturday, this strange day of questions and confusion? I know of no hymns written for Holy Saturday. Oddly, too, there is no reason for the congregation to gather together. Holy Saturday is a lonely day for Christians.

Theology must take the death of Jesus seriously. Rightly, we must not be in too much of a rush to get from Holy Saturday to Easter Sunday for fear of minimizing the awfulness of what has happened. Even on resurrection morning Jesus is no less the crucified Lord, always bearing the scars of his scourging and the piercings of his crucifixion. Jesus' death was deadly. Like the disciples, we must wait in dark despair a day longer. The continuance of death marks the end of Holy Week.

HOLY SATURDAY IS NOT THE LAST WORD

However, unlike the disciples, from our present perspective we know the story does not end with Holy Saturday. That knowledge blunts the sharp point of the commemoration of Jesus' death and takes away some of the terrible emptiness and ambiguity of Holy Saturday. A theology of glory waits impatiently in the wings, eager for center stage. The truth is that the ontological emptiness of Holy Saturday is piously dismissed by efficient ecclesiastical and liturgical planning. We are already leaning into Easter Sunday. The lilies are put in place as chancel decorations, eager in their symbolic way to trumpet the good news. The white paraments are placed over the bare wood of the pulpit and Communion table. The choir has already rehearsed the Easter anthem. The resurrection sermon is written, perhaps to be gone over one last time. And, to seal the fact that we have not really entered into the terrible nothing of Holy Saturday, the bulletins for Sunday morning are sitting on the ledge in the narthex awaiting distribution when the people arrive. And there, unobtrusively beside the bulletins, is the Paschal candle and a box of matches, for the Easter service begins with the entrance of the candle, lit once again, to signal the resurrected Jesus as the light of the world. I am told that in the United States this day is one of the busiest shopping days of the year!

From our present perspective, Holy Saturday is an "almost" sort of day. In one regard the atonement is complete, but the victory is not yet won, and the vindication of the Son by the Father is not yet asserted. We lean forward hopefully, knowingly, but as yet there is no power and, of course, no basis for joy and no ground for hope. Until the appearances by the risen Jesus, the disciples hid, furtive and fearful. Without the resurrection appearances they could not yet know the meaning of what really had happened on Good Friday and, to their coming astonishment, what was yet to happen on all of the following days of the rest of their lives. On Holy Saturday all that Jesus had said and done could not yet compete with his death. Death still had its sting. Death apparently held the victory. The religious and moral influence of a dead man of God was a pyrrhic victory at best. Jesus was dead. The dream was over. Once they got over the shock of the violence and shame of Jesus' crucifixion, the disciples would be ready to go back to work to earn an honest living. It had been an interesting three years, no doubt. But life must go on.

Unlike the disciples, however, we know the story, especially its end. As I see it, right here, however, is the complex ambiguity that frames the experience of faith and ministry for many of us: knowing the end of the story, and even having planned for Easter Day, we remain stuck with the experience of the mood of Holy Saturday. We have not yet entered into the reality of Christian life in terms of Easter Sunday.

PROBLEMS WITH MINISTRY IN THE
MOOD OF HOLY SATURDAY

Why this is the case is difficult to explain. There is something of "living between the times" about it. The victory is won, but the battle is not yet over. Eternal life is promised, but we still get sick and die. Jesus lives and reigns, but the cruelty and suffering in the world remain undiminished. In our own lives we confess our faith, yet we often feel trapped in our moral confusions and stuck in our attempts to live holy lives. We speak of the gift of the Holy Spirit to the church, while we limp along apologetically, with long faces and sour dispositions. For all of our preaching and teaching, nothing much seems to change in the lives of the people—at least that is how it feels on our darker days. Jesus may be raised from the dead, but we remain still the people of Holy Saturday, looking longingly across the divide that takes us to Easter Day, praying wistfully for the power of the Holy Spirit.

Ministry in the space between Holy Saturday and Easter Sunday is an "almost" sort of ministry. The mood of Holy Saturday has become a metaphor for our experience. We know the story, but we have not caught up with Easter Sunday. Somewhere along the way the power and the joy and the wonder got lost. Ministry as doxology was squashed, perhaps, by the obligations of relentless duty. Joy came to be squeezed out by weariness. Everything is prepared for ministry in the mood of Easter Sunday, but the day itself seemingly has not arrived. The eschatological clock appears to have stopped. Ministry in the mood of Holy Saturday is ministry filled with ambiguity, Janus-like, looking backward and forward, but somehow stuck.

The contrast between ministry in the mood of Holy Saturday and ministry in the mood of Easter Sunday is illustrated by the comparison of Jesus' disciples before the Easter appearances and after the ascension. During the evening of the day of resurrection they were huddled together in fear in a locked house (John 20:19). They did not yet know that Jesus had risen from death. After the ascension, on the other hand, they returned to Jerusalem "with great joy; and they were continually in the temple blessing God" (Luke 24:52-53).

Consider the following contrasts: inward looking self-preservation versus expansive, outgoing evangelism; return to the old days versus a new, hitherto unimaginable future; grief versus joy; doubt versus praise; fearfulness and hiding versus courage that goes public, defying the judicial injunction to remain silent (Acts 4:18-20); disbelief versus conviction; confusion versus clarity. In sum, "God help us" versus "Hallelujah, Jesus lives." To put this in pastoral terms, the contrast is between ministry focused on ourselves—missional timidity and ecclesiastical maintenance that protects and preserves what we have, with a vague though uncertain hope for continued life—or ministry that bursts forth in creative, overflowing desire to tell the world, "Jesus is risen!" Imagine the astonished newspaper headline: "Church Affirms Jesus Is Alive, and Lives Believing It's True." It is the difference between ministry without power, because everything is left up to us to do, leaving us anxious and exhausted, and ministry filled with joy and hope because the Lord not only lives but also reigns and acts in power for us.

THE RESURRECTION OF JESUS' MINISTRY

Clearly then the resurrection of ministry is not first of all about new life for our ministries. Neither is it a metaphor for getting ministry kick-started again because of a newfound attitude or program of ministry renewal. I am after something much more radical than these proposals, worthy and legitimate as they are, no doubt. My argument is that the resurrection of ministry is first of all about the resurrection of *Jesus'* ministry. Because Jesus is raised, he not only has a new life but his ministry has a new future. Jesus raised and ascended, with work to do, is the basis for joy and the ground for hope, as much with regard to ministry as it is with regard to faith.

This book then is an unabashed practical theology of the Easter Lord. It is a practical theology of glory because it is a book about Jesus, resurrected, acting and reigning! Thus we must speak of the resurrection *and* the ascension of Jesus. Theology over the recent decades has rightly and helpfully attended to the suffering God. Theodicy is much on our minds. We have learned again that a Christian theology is always a theology of the cross. God with us and for us in, through and as Jesus Christ in the midst of humanity's agony is the gospel for all who suffer. We have been rightly warned away from a *theologia gloriae* when the emphasis is placed on the church triumphant. Luther's *theologia crucis* protects the church from facile optimism and empty triumphalism, while leading us to recognize knowledge of God and his salvation through the cross of Calvary.

Perhaps, however, for fear of holding up to view a God who has not plumbed the depths of human sin and pain, we have been slow to attest the triumph of God, not only through the cross but especially through the resurrection of Jesus. Perhaps the *dénouement* of the gospel account of Jesus of Nazareth has been felt to be a bit of an embarrassment for us in our time, just too much to believe in such an age both enchanted by scientific success and yet characterized by loss of conviction. Perhaps the resurrection of Jesus has been elided into a lovely, hope-filled metaphor, but in the process its reality and power for joy and hope have been put aside. The gospel, however, is not a metaphor but a personal, living Lord. Perhaps too the resurrection has come to be interpreted as more about us and what we feel than about Jesus and something that happened to him. Whatever the reasons for loss of joy and hope in present Christian experience, and especially in the experience of many people involved in ministry, it is right to risk aggressive movement to reclaim the centrality of the resurrection and ascension of Jesus for our Christian consciousness and practice.

THE RESURRECTION OF OUR MINISTRY

The resurrection of Jesus *demands* the resurrection of ministry from the mood of Holy Saturday for the reason that Easter Sunday and Ascension Thursday mean the resurrection and continuance of Jesus' ministry. Maybe that statement needs to be put more sharply: apart from Jesus' continuing ministry the church has no ministry whatsoever. But because Jesus has a resurrected ministry, we have a ministry that is entirely oriented around his living ministry. However, this is more than putting our ministry into a new perspective. It is a foundational realignment of ministry. Henceforth, everything must be cast in terms of what it means for us to share in Jesus' living ministry.

The crucifixion of ministry has its rightful place as the displacement of our messianic pretensions, and we cannot forget that there is no Easter Day without Good Friday (the theme of my book *The Crucifixion of Ministry*). In this sequel, I take the next step, where the accent is on joy, and the horizon of meaning is filled with hope and the expectation both of charismatic giftedness for the church and God's ultimate triumph over the forces that make for death and evil. The awareness of the victory of God in the resurrection of Jesus is deliberately and without apology sharp and all-embracing. The focus, as always, is on Jesus, and therefore on what his life and ministry as the resurrected and ascended Lord mean for us. What is his ministry in its resurrection and ascension aspects? And what does our ministry (and faith) look like in the mood of Easter Sunday and Ascension Thursday? This last question is critical, of course, because the life and ministry of the resurrected Jesus is not just a pleasing theological idea, but directs us to a compelling participation in a living fellowship that surely shapes and informs everything that we do. What follows is my attempt to answer these questions by giving a positive statement of the resurrected and ascended life and ministry of Jesus Christ, and of our ministry in view of that.

Along the way I will bring in illustrations of what I think this ministry looks like. I call them steps on the way from ministry in the mood of Holy Saturday to ministry in the mood of Easter Sunday. I envision what faith and ministry look like when we move from the mood of Holy Saturday to the joy and hope of Easter Sunday, and, to be complete, and central to the account, to our sharing in the Lord's ministry following Ascension Thursday. What follows then is a pastoral theology of Easter Day and Ascension Thursday as we explore what it means to live in the victory of God won in, through and as Jesus Christ.

> Turn again, O God, and quicken us,
> That your people may rejoice in you.
> Make us clean hearts, O God,
> And renew a right spirit within us.

Give us again the joy of your help.
With your Spirit of freedom sustain us.
Though Jesus Christ, our living and reigning Lord.
Amen.

1

IT'S NOT ABOUT
THE RESURRECTION BUT
JESUS RISEN AND REIGNING

THE ACTUALITY OF THE RESURRECTION of Jesus from the dead, and his subsequent ascension and ministry at the right hand of the Father and through the Holy Spirit, make Christian faith and ministry possible. Christian faith and ministry are the direct consequences of what happened to Jesus, as God the Holy Spirit joins us to him to share in his life, and therefore also in his ministry. Joy and hope, therefore, mark Christian identity because Jesus the Christ is risen, reigns and will come again, and we, in union with him, share now in his life. If Jesus is not raised and we are not joined to his life, faith and ministry are in vain. In which case, the experience that results is not joy and hope, but weariness and despair. Faith has no ground, no basis and no source in God. And ministry is without power.

The main goal of this chapter is to chart the initial steps that take us from ministry in the mood of Holy Saturday to ministry in the mood of Easter Sunday.

IT'S ABOUT JESUS

It's about Jesus! Sometimes the obvious is so obvious and taken for granted that it is lost sight of altogether. It is the proverbial "not seeing the trees for the forest." That can certainly happen in theology when we get caught up in complex constructions and qualifications. So let us begin with the obvious: Jesus is the subject matter of Christian faith, and Jesus, living and reigning, is the subject matter of the resurrection and the ascension. To confess that Jesus is Lord entails not only that Jesus lives but that he lives for a purpose. We will get to what this means in due course. But let us be clear on this first point: Jesus lives! Everything else follows as a result of this confession and the truth it bears witness to.

Notice I have not used *Christ* and *God* while insisting that Christian faith is foundationally about Jesus, living and reigning. Of course these words are very important, and each must be given its proper place in the expression of Christian faith. But the truth of Christian faith, and therefore of Christian ministry, is not located in the first instance in a theological title—in "Christ"—nor in a general concept of deity—"God." The truth for Christian faith and ministry is located in the personal particularity of Jesus, who in the flesh of his humanity is both Christ and God. Let me very briefly explain something of what is involved in these assertions.

Jesus, not a Christ principle. The theological title "Christ" has, I think, a largely ambiguous meaning and reference for many people today. But the real theological problem with the word arises when it gets separated from Jesus, and is used alone. Too easily, then, it may get detached from its anchor in Jewish theological history, and its fulfillment in and as the man Jesus. The concept of Christ can too readily turn into a Christ principle, becoming a general concept or idea that has slipped its moorings, namely, the particularity of the man Jesus, who is Christ.

Separated from Jesus, the word *Christ* tends to assume a docetic leaning as an abstract personal noun. When we speak of Christ without conscious awareness that we are speaking of Jesus, his humanity may slip away from our thinking. Speaking about Jesus, who was fully God, reminds us that he was and is a man. Even as the resurrected Lord, Jesus never ceases to be fully human. As such, he, our high priest, ever lives to be the mediator between the Father and us, bringing God to us and us to God, all in the power of the Holy Spirit. When we lose hold on his humanity, everything gets cast back on us to establish a relationship with God. Then we are on the road to reintroducing messianic pretensions into our Christian practice. Even as the title of "Christ" and the history of expectation that preceded it identify Jesus as the Lord's anointed, it is Jesus, finally, who gives the title its full meaning. The title is transformed as Jesus and the history he lived and lives reconstitute its meaning. Because he is singularly the incarnate Lord, the word *Christ* has proper use and appropriate meaning only when attached to the person of Jesus in the flesh of his humanity. Speaking of Jesus, then, helps keep us theologically grounded.

Jesus, not a general concept of God. The word *God* is especially problematic because of its wide use (whether as blessing or curse) and the assumption thereby that we actually know who we are talking about. The theological danger lies again in an abstract general concept, in this case, of a generic God of the religions, lying behind the back of Jesus, as it were, or behind the doctrine of the holy Trinity. This general concept of God is seen to be applicable to all religions and may have also a civil religious reference. The Christian doctrine of God, then, becomes a particular instance of a general concept. The implication is devastating for Christian faith. Father, Son and Holy Spirit can no longer be seen to be the name of God. God, as the trinitarian communion of love, becomes a Christian addition, but cannot be seen to be intrinsic to God. It is impossible then to get from a general religious concept of God to a proper theological understanding of Jesus as Lord.

Because Jesus is God, the concept of God itself has to undergo a profound reconstruction from an essentially unitarian monotheism to the doctrine of the Trinity. Two verses of Scripture especially inform us, showing how the concept of God itself has to be christologically controlled. First, it is the Son, "who is close to the Father's heart, who has made him known" (in Greek, who has exegeted him! [John 1:18]). And second, Jesus tells us that "no one knows the Son except the Father, and no one knows the Father except the Son and anyone to whom the Son chooses to reveal him" (Matthew 11:27). The Reformer John Calvin advised that "God is comprehended in Christ alone" (*Institutes of the Christian Religion* 2.6.4). At the risk of using an inappropriately startling image to make a theological point: there is a kind of christologically necessitated atheism here in the repeated "no one" in Matthew's verse.

Christian faith is genuinely radical and appropriately scandalous to the general religious imagination, just as it is nonsensical to the secular equivalent, precisely because of its astonishing and insistent historical particularity. It is a faith that deals with Jesus, born through Mary's birth canal, acknowledging that he is the Christ, and confessing that he is wholly and fully God. Our understanding of both *Christ* and *God* are filled in by Jesus, by who he was and is, by what he did and does, by what he said and says, and by what happened to him.

FIRST STEP: FOCUS ON JESUS

Although we have not gone far in our theological journey, already the scenery around us invites a brief reflection on ministry. As we move from ministry in the mood of Holy Saturday to ministry in the mood of Easter Sunday, the crucial first step is to focus on Jesus rather than on a Christ principle or a general concept of God. Taking this step orientates the practice of ministry and gives it specific content. The radical claim of Christian faith is that Jesus is God. The hidden God became a human person. The incomprehensible God made himself known in, through and as this man, Jesus, and to be for us no other than this. As Jesus, and in the Spirit, God dealt and deals with us. But we cannot allow ourselves to speak of Jesus only in the past tense. Because he is risen and ascended, we must also speak of him in the present tense. As Jesus, and in the Spirit, God still deals with us. And we, dealing with Jesus, are dealing with God.

The conclusion drawn from this is that through Jesus, God is known to be a relational and therefore personal God. And although these terms invite fuller discussion, it is because we know what it means to be in personal relationships that we have some sense of what it must mean to think of God and our life in God in such terms.

Often the pastoral need, whatever the presenting issue, is for the affirmation of a personal God who draws close, whose name we know, whose way with us is love and mercy, and whose goal is to bring us home to himself. To a parishioner paralyzed by the notion of an angry God of judgment, we hold out Jesus. While we do not avoid the time to speak of sin and God's judgment, we always do so in terms of Jesus, in whom God is known to be lovingly and graciously personal and relational rather than implacably angry and eternally condemning. To a parishioner who has lost a sense, an awareness, of God, and for whom God is felt to be absent in the time of a difficult season in life, we hold out Jesus. While we do not avoid taking time to listen with receptivity and care to expressions of spiritual despair, we do so trusting that in the Spirit Jesus is in fact at hand and at work to bless, to comfort and to heal, because that is who God is and what God does. To the parishioner for whom a theological perspective is angrily defended by propositions and argument, and who brings divisiveness and rancor into the Christian community, we hold out Jesus. While we most certainly affirm the need for careful theology, and reject theology that is not faithful to the gospel, we do so telling of a Jesus who as personal being cannot be contained in our statements or prescribed by our arguments.

We hold out Jesus because we know he lives. We speak of him, trusting that in the freedom of his love and by the grace and agency of the Holy Spirit, Jesus gives himself to his people. Undoubtedly we confront a great mystery when we speak of the Lord's presence, and our language must reflect that. Nonetheless, in ministry we place our trust in a living and acting Lord, present through the agency of the Holy Spirit, and here is the point: we know his name and we know his work. His name is Jesus and his work is loving reconciliation with the Father.

We need a rewritten road map. We have an odd saying in Pittsburgh, where I live and teach, which slightly scrambles a familiar colloquialism: "You can't get from here to there." Pittsburgh is a town of hills, tunnels, rivers and bridges. On any day, it seems, a major traffic artery, tunnel or bridge is under reconstruction, or one of the three rivers has overflowed a bank somewhere, closing off an exit or access ramp. Wags say that the state tree in Pennsylvania is the orange and white construction barrier! And because of these three rivers, everything geographic is triangulated. I know where I want to go, but I cannot get from here to there.

The biblical equivalent of driving in Pittsburgh, perhaps, is Luke 24:5. The women brought their prepared spices to the tomb of Jesus. They, no doubt, were astonished to find the stone rolled away from the entrance to the tomb. Entering, they did not find Jesus' body. The perplexed women suddenly found two men in dazzling clothes standing beside them, and were terrified, bowing their faces to the ground. The men asked them, "Why do you look for the living among the dead?" They were looking for Jesus in the wrong place. The women wanted to find Jesus, but they had no access ramp to take them there, even if they knew where to find him. Given their frame of reference, they can't get from here to there. The road map of faith will have to be totally rewritten in view of the event that unfolded and the events yet to occur. The women have no way to get from the empty tomb to the risen Lord. Until the Lord encounters them, there is no answer to the question put by the angels.

From Pittsburgh to the Emmaus Road. The need for a rewritten road map of faith is given narrative expression in the familiar account of the two disciples walking from Jerusalem to the village of Emmaus, a journey of seven miles. They were in conversation about the arrest, trial and execution of Jesus. Somewhere along the road the risen Jesus joined them. They were unable to recognize him, apparently by divine act. The incognito that characterized him in the flesh also characterized him in his appearances. Jesus asked what they were talking about. Undoubtedly surprised at his apparent ignorance, one of them, Cleopas, asked if he was the only stranger in Jerusalem who did not know the events of the past days. The assumption appears to be that the arrest, trial and execution of Jesus from Nazareth was headline news, the prime subject of the Jerusalem equivalent of water-cooler conversation. They explained to their traveling companion the events that had taken place during the past days and who had been executed. They moved from sadness to confusion as their explanation of the events unfolded. They had hoped Jesus was the one who would redeem Israel. And besides, they said, some of the women of the group who went to anoint the body of the dead prophet found the tomb empty. Further, the women appeared to have had a conversation with two angels, who told them that this Jesus was alive. Some of the others went to the tomb after the women told them their story. They too found it empty. Confusion reigned, it seems.

The narrator now inserts dramatic words from Jesus. "Oh, how foolish you are, and how slow of heart to believe all that the prophets have declared! Was it not necessary that the Messiah should suffer these things and then enter his glory?" (Luke 24:25-26). It seems he was a bit impatient with his companions. Nevertheless, he then goes on to expound the promissory history of God with Israel that prepared the way for his coming and the history that would follow. But still, for all this, they did not recognize him. He remained incognito.

The exposition done, Jesus walked on ahead to the village. Hospitably, and still unaware of the identity of their traveling companion, the two disciples urged Jesus to join them for the evening meal and stay the night as their guest. At table, Jesus began a ritual that was suddenly familiar: he took bread, blessed and broke it, and gave it to them. Their eyes were opened and they recognized him, whereupon he vanished from their sight. Almost anticlimactically, they say to each other that while Jesus was explaining the Scriptures their hearts burned within them.

Within the hour the experience settled and they began to grasp that something utterly momentous had happened, although as yet they hardly had the categories to understand it. One can only imagine the thrill, the confusion, the wonder, the astonishment, the giddy excitement that these two men must have felt. Everything in their lives, surely, had just been turned upside down. Something of this is suggested, I think, in the urgent immediacy of their response: they got up, tired as they must have been, and walked all the seven miles back to Jerusalem to the house of the gathered eleven and their companions. They gave an account of their experience, of the exposition of Scripture and the breaking of the bread, and how suddenly they recognized at last the identity of their traveling companion.

As this was going on, interrupting their narrative, Jesus himself suddenly stood among them. This was the irruption of the unfamiliar into the familiar. "Peace be with you," he said. But they were startled and terrified, for they thought they were seeing a ghost. Jesus reassured them that it was he. But they remained disbelieving, even in their joy. The subsequent prosaic request for food was the intrusion of the familiar into the unfamiliar.

Let me stop the rendering of the account to make note again of two key points. First, the disciples had no experience of the resurrection as such, but of the resurrected Jesus—and that really is much more important. Even so, as yet they had no conceptual apparatus by which to understand what was happening. Not until *he* opened their minds did they begin the process of understanding. Second, the disciples knew that Jesus was alive because he is the Lord who has encountered them. The focus was not on metaphysics, by which the event of the resurrection or the appearance of an apparently resurrected person might be explained or understood; the focus was on personal encounter by a living Lord who stood among them so that they would subsequently witnesses to the truth: Jesus has risen from the tomb! How this happened is just not a question of even casual concern. But what it means demands a complete rewriting of the road map of faith if the disciples are to get from here to there.

SECOND STEP: REWRITING THE ROAD MAP OF MINISTRY
To move from ministry in the mood of Holy Saturday to ministry

in the mood of Easter Sunday we too will have to rewrite the road map of faith. Specifically, we will need to rewrite the road map of ministry. Let me suggest now a second step to take: a willingness to admit that some rewriting is required, and we must get concrete about this. If the first step to take was crucial, the need to deal with Jesus, this second step is urgent. If we refuse to take this second step, ministry in the continuing mood of Holy Saturday will sooner or later leave us burned out, dispirited and depressed for this reason: it is not faithful to the reality that is at the core of faith and ministry. That core: *Jesus lives.*

Rewriting is a pain. Everyone who faces a blank computer screen and begins to write knows that rewriting will be necessary at some point. Sermons, for example, take hard writing and re-writing. Thoughtful prayers for public worship need to be crafted and recrafted. Thinking about the central issues of Christian faith too leads to revision, and now and then even the transformation of our minds (Romans 12:2). We grasp the things of God dimly, and only by hard study may we grasp them somewhat less dimly. Our spiritual lives, often fragile and shallow-rooted, periodically need to be reclaimed or rerooted. Maybe, in a sense, we can even speak of the need sometimes for reconversion. At the very least recommitment, the fruit of repentance, demands our attention with season-like regularity.

If we feel stuck in the mood of Holy Saturday, the road map of ministry will need to be rewritten, and that too involves hard work. For whatever the reason—drift, lack of critical reflection on practice, getting started with and then stuck with a poorly con-structed theology of ministry, a season of spiritual laziness, the overwhelming pressure of expectations—periodically ministry needs to be rethought. Some of these images also apply to minis-try: ministry rewritten, recrafted, reclaimed, rerooted, recommitted. Some hard, perhaps scary, questions may indicate that some kind of malaise has set in and that something needs to be done about it, urgently. What do I do for fifty-some hours a week? Why has sermon preparation become such drudgery? What happened to the sparkle and hope I felt on the day of my ordination? Why does nothing change unless I put my back into it? Where did my feelings of resentment toward my congregation come from? What happened to my prayer life? When did I last read a decent book on theology, a book that pushed me, a book that changed how I think about God? Do I really think another book on developing more pragmatic skills for ministry will turn things around? Why am I always so tired?

These questions are only suggestive, of course. But if it feels as though ministry is trapped in the mood of Holy Saturday, ministry is indeed in urgent need of being reframed. The core problem, perhaps the terrifying problem, is there is no Christian faith on Holy Saturday and no possibility for Christian ministry because all we have at that point is Jesus as a dead moral and religious influence. He "lives" only as a particular instance of a general religious memory and impulse. Faith does not apply in such a circumstance. Even knowing what happened on the following day, if we remain stuck in the mood of Holy Saturday we have separated ourselves from the resurrection joy and hope of the Easter Lord. All we have is a huge burden to carry because at this point everything seems to be left up to us to do. It is little wonder, then, that we are always weary.

I recall a student taking a class with me on classical texts in pastoral theology. He was a working pastor in a large, busy, multi-staff congregation, finishing seminary on a part-time basis. He had been in ministry a number of years. We read books by Gregory of Nazianzus, John Chrysostom, Gregory the Great, Martin

Bucer and Richard Baxter. Judging from what he told me, at the start of the term he did not think there was much of a problem in his ministry, and he certainly did not expect a course on ancient pastoral texts to cause any uproar. But as he worked his way through these old books, awareness slowly dawned: his ministry had lost its theological and spiritual center. By mid-term he was agitated. The crisis deepened. By the end of term he wrote me a paper in which he showed how these books—on one level dry and nonpractical, representing thinking about ministry from the fourth, sixth, sixteenth and seventeenth centuries—had opened his eyes to a whole new perspective on ministry. His paper was his rewritten road map for ministry arising out of his conversation with long-dead master pastors. He finished the course as a pastor who had refound his center, his theological identity and his vocation once more.

THE CENTRAL PERSPECTIVE: THE CENTRAL PARADOX

The resurrection of Jesus is the central perspective of the New Testament. It is the lens through which everything is viewed, backward and forward. The story of redemption is written from the conviction that the once dead Jesus is now alive again in a new way. "If Christ has not been raised, your faith [and ministry] is futile" (1 Corinthians 15:17). We have been given a "new birth into a living hope through the resurrection of Jesus" (1 Peter 1:3). We share in Jesus' resurrection so that we might walk in newness of life (Romans 6:4). Likewise, the resurrection of Jesus is central to the church's confession: "On the third day he rose again." Christian faith is, by the Holy Spirit, faith in, a relationship with and sharing in the ministry of the living Lord. We will try to understand something of what all of this means as we look at the resurrected Jesus from a number of angles. This, however, is no easy task. Let us look briefly at one difficulty.

The importance and centrality of the resurrection of Jesus can hardly be overstated. Nevertheless, what we must deal with here is not really an event but a person. And that makes our thinking about him all the harder. While at best the creeds of the church, properly understood, have been able to confess and protect the central mystery of Jesus' personal identity while on earth, tight definition has remained elusive. Certainly there is the empirical component of his humanity to anchor the attempts to understand Jesus' personal identity in something resembling human experience and identity. However, while his consubstantial unity with the Father can be confessed, it remains the deepest mystery. With respect to the resurrected Jesus, however, all of our conceptual categories are broken open. Now our earthbound thinking is shattered, for the resurrection—or better, the risen Lord—is beyond all human conceiving. Certainly the empty tomb is an empirical correlate to the resurrection, but it hardly fills in our understanding of the resurrected *Jesus*. To illustrate this from one perspective: in his appearances we encounter a body—and without doubt Jesus is embodied—not subject to our experience of space and time. This defies explanation within our understanding of created time and space. The problem is not that we must try to think the impossible but that we must try to think the ineffable. If we think of space and time as the box within which we live and think, thinking about the resurrected Jesus means, literally, thinking outside the box.

So here is the central paradox that confronts us when we try to think about the resurrected Jesus: he is the central perspective from which all of Christian faith is determined, yet we have no human categories of thought by which to bring him to expression. The sentence, "The resurrected Jesus is like . . ." cannot be completed. Easily we can say that we have before us a mystery to be adored rather than a problem to be solved, and that is a true statement. At the very least it might cause us to drop to our knees in wonder and worship.

SPEAKING ABOUT THE RESURRECTED JESUS

Our incapacity at this point, however, is not the end of the matter. In general, it is no trivial matter to try to speak faithfully concerning God. "To whom then will you liken God, or what likeness compare with him? . . . [W]ho is my equal, says the Holy One?" (Isaiah 40:18, 25) "*No one* knows the Son except the Father; and *no one* knows the Father except the Son" (Matthew 11:27, emphasis added). On the other hand, in Christian faith we believe that God has given himself to be known by us by accommodating himself to our creaturely ways of thinking and speaking. So the text from Isaiah is rightly balanced by the central affirmation from John: "the Word became flesh and lived among us" (John 1:14), and the verse from Matthew 11 continues "and anyone to whom the Son chooses to reveal him." It is, as it were, as if Jesus takes us by the hand and leads us to knowledge and speech of the Father. Or, in a different image, he speaks himself and God into our minds. Just as a child learns speech by being spoken to by his or her parents, as we are spoken to by Jesus we are able to bring him, and indeed God, to appropriate speech. Jesus, as it were, speaks himself into our speaking of him.

Jesus spoke forth himself while on earth. Jesus also spoke forth himself during the forty days between the resurrection and the ascension. Jesus speaks forth himself today as the ascended Lord, not now limited by the created categories of time and space. He speaks forth himself by the Holy Spirit, especially through the proclamation of the sermon. Jesus also will speak forth himself as the end (as the *eschatos*) when he gathers all things together and gives them to the Father. Theological speech is possible therefore on the grounds of Jesus bearing witness to himself through the Holy Spirit and of our being converted in the structures of our thinking and developing speech that has its sole ground in him. This in part is what is meant when Paul tells us that we have the mind of Christ (1 Corinthians 2:16). Thus can we speak of the risen and ascended Lord. Such speaking is our "rational worship" (see Romans 12:1-2) in which we acknowledge that we speak as we are spoken to by the risen Word who bears witness to himself.

Speech concerning the resurrected Jesus is confessional speech, the speech of faith. There are no outside references or independent warrants we can appeal to. Faith speaks to faith, and the Holy Spirit alone can open the ears if another would also hear (cf. Psalm 40:6).

THIRD STEP: BECOMING THEOLOGIANS

Our discussion suggests a necessary third step to take in the move from ministry in the mood of Holy Saturday to ministry in the mood of Easter Sunday: claim the responsibility to be a theologian. At first glance this may not appear to be the most practical advice. But in fulfilling our responsibility to *know* the resurrected and ascended Lord, and out of that knowledge to teach and preach the gospel, our minds must be filled with something resembling competent, thoughtful, and informed theology. We cannot practice ministry without the work of doing theology. Thus, to repeat what others have also said, if you want to become a faithful pastor, become a hard-working theologian.

A theologian, said early church theologian Evagrius Ponticus, is someone who prays. Let us think of prayer expansively, beyond what we say to God. Let us think of prayer as including giving attention to what God says to us. Perhaps then the aphorism may be rewritten: a theologian is someone who listens to God, and out of that listening thinks and speaks faithfully. The first work of theology is prayer in the widest sense.

Karl Barth, at the beginning of his massive *Church Dogmatics*, defined dogmatics as the work that the church does to test its preaching against the gospel. This takes us right to the heart of things. Without the work of theology our preaching becomes lazy, no matter the homiletical skill at our command. People, I believe, do not just want or need to hear biblical texts rightly interpreted. They do not just want or need counsel to guide their living. They do not just want or need winsome, well-illustrated delivery. Something more radical is required: they want and need God to encounter them in the sermon.

What is required of us then is a commitment to God for the sake of the people that we will, with God's help, become theologians. To be godly theologians we will retire often from the office to the study. We will forsake (some of) the meetings for the sake of theological work. We will be less busy to do greater proclamation. We will reclaim what we were ordained to do: Word and sacraments, with energy, intelligence, imagination and love.

THE RESURRECTION: A SINGULAR EVENT
THAT HAPPENED TO JESUS

Our topic is not the resurrection as such, but Jesus, who is resurrected and ascended, and who is the Lord who encounters us. The resurrection is ultimately of interest insofar as it was something that happened to Jesus. It was a singular theological event (a God event) in consequence of a singular death to a singular person. I have no interest in it otherwise. Let me expand on this by making five brief points.

First, the resurrection of Jesus was a new creation, a singular event, and is not to be regarded as a general category of potential human experience, as was taught for example by the Pharisees of Jesus' time. It was a singular event within the Father-Son relationship and remains shrouded, therefore, in the trinitarian mystery of the Godhead. Within history as we perceive it, there has been only one resurrection: the resurrection of Jesus. "I believe in the resurrection of the body," as we say in the creed, has a specific reference to Jesus before it has any general reference to us as the goal of Christian hope. It is the particular, his resurrection, that is the ground for the general, our resurrection, not the other way around. That is to say, our future resurrection is tied at all points to Jesus' resurrection and therefore to him, and is possible only on that basis.

Second, with the resurrection of Jesus something utterly new entered into history. The resurrected Jesus' appearances happened in time and space. There is, then, a stubborn historicity to the resurrection of Jesus. Yet these events do not belong to the series of events that make history in the sense that we cannot understand the resurrection in terms of them. There was no process, no contingent causality, as there must be with every other event in history. We are bound to something that happened once. This singularity means the end of history in one sense, as a closed continuum of cause and effect, for history now is opened up into a new horizon of hope that hitherto was not possible. That is to say, henceforth history must be understood out of a center in the resurrected Jesus rather than the resurrected Jesus out of a prior concept of history, which in any case is impossible. This means a revolution in our concept of history. More will be said on this matter later.

Third, the resurrection is to be regarded as a part of Jesus' personal experience. As resurrected, new life was and is part of his life, and as resurrected life it is part of his continuing and future history. Perhaps we must go on to say that the resurrection is the ground of Jesus' new experience of life in the body of flesh, because his is now an embodiment and indeed a humanity that utterly transcends his (and our) prior experience of being human.

Fourth, because of the singularity of Jesus' resurrection in his body—in the flesh of his humanity and continuing with this body, but now without limits of created time and space as we experience them—all after-life theories are now without merit, carry no theological interest and certainly have no place in Christian thinking. For example, the New Testament does not teach that the disembodied soul of Jesus left the decaying corpse and flew off to somewhere ("the angel in the slot machine theory"). The resurrected Jesus was and is an embodied person. The witness of the forty days is a deep mystery, no doubt, though compounded, I suggest, precisely by Jesus' resurrected kind of physicality.

Allow me a comment on what I have just written. I have found through the years that the resurrection of the body is often a shocking notion for many people, at times even deeply offensive, when they take a moment to think about it. Others, perhaps, hear the words but seem not to grasp the consequences. In either case, at issue, I assume, is the seeming fact that the doctrine of the immortality of the soul is embedded in the Western mind, perhaps ineradicably. The singularity of Jesus' bodily resurrection and its meaning call into question all our extant definitions of life after death. This is not only an uncomfortable topic of discourse; the prospect or otherwise of life after death is also fraught with anxiety and fear. Rightly, I suppose, many people do not want their eschatological comfort disturbed. If the notion of the immortality of the soul is to survive as a Christian doctrine, it will need to be overhauled quite thoroughly in specifically Christian, that is, christological, which means embodied, terms.

Fifth, the resurrection of Jesus means the actuality of his ministry in a new way. While the subject is the same Jesus, the resurrection means the advent of a new ministry for him. This is not a ministry different in content or goal from Jesus' earthly ministry, but it is a ministry different in kind because he is now present to us in the Holy Spirit. As resurrected in his humanity, there are now no spatial or temporal limits to constrain him, at least as we experience and in some way understand them. Further, there is now no death in his future, as there was while he lived on earth. And as on earth he was the recipient of the Holy Spirit, now in heaven he is, from the Father, the giver of himself as and through the Holy Spirit. (The *filioque* doctrine of the Western church seems to me to assert a christological dimension and content to the sending of the Spirit that the Eastern church lacks at this point.) From the Father, through the Son and in the Holy Spirit: this now is the ground of the church's ministry. To the Father, through the Son and in the Holy Spirit: this now is the goal of the church's ministry.

These five points, however, may be tempered by a caveat. Drawing on my own Reformed tradition for guidance, I was happy to find these words from John Calvin, who advocated a cautious approach, calling for "some suggestion of the manner of the resurrection. I use this language," he wrote, "because Paul, calling it 'a mystery,' urges us to sobriety and restrains us from philosophizing too freely and subtly" (*Institutes* 3.25.8). We should also approach our topic with restraint, humility and respect, seeking to speak worthily of this act of heaven upon the Lord Jesus.

2

STARTING FROM THE ASCENSION

The Lord Who Encounters Us

IN CHAPTER ONE I SUGGESTED three steps to take that move us from ministry in the mood of Holy Saturday to ministry in the mood of Easter Sunday. In this chapter I want to emphasize that these steps are in response to the Lord, who, in the Holy Spirit, takes the first step. He encounters us. We are dealt with by God, just as others are dealt with by God. We are encountered by God again and again as the living Lord acts in the Spirit in our lives. My supposition is that we would not be in ministry otherwise. Each of us can recount the experience of being called into ministry: the circumstances, the people involved, the testing, perhaps the resistance and the years of preparation. We can also recount the continuing sense that God acts through us. With the eyes of faith we see miracles, lives changed, people blessed.

The other side of this, however, is that we don't always *feel* dealt with by God. The joy of faith is countered by doubts; seasons of theological clarity give way to seasons when knowledge of God seem to be especially dim. In ministry there are times when God

seems far removed from the exercise of our responsibilities. The
sermon bank appears to be empty of deposits. We are afflicted
with lassitude. Nothing much changes in the congregation in spite
of our preaching and teaching and counseling. Miracles don't
seem to happen any more. When we feel like this, we are trapped
in the mood and the experience of Holy Saturday.

The word we need to have spoken into this situation is the reminder that God acts; specifically in, through and as Jesus and in
the Spirit, God acts. This is shrouded in deepest mystery. That
God acts in, through and as the living Jesus is the great master
narrative of the New Testament.

JESUS IS AN ACTIVE LORD

As the risen and ascended Lord, Jesus does not now sit in heaven
with his arms folded waiting for us to do something religious that
he can affirm (an image from Karl Barth). Jesus is not our cheer-
leader from the heavens hoping we will get faith and ministry
right. Neither does Jesus want to get more involved in *our* ministries. Why would he? Our ministries are not redemptive. We don't
raise the dead, forgive the sinful, heal the sick or bring in the reign
of God. Rather, Jesus has his own resurrected ministry to do—
raising the dead, forgiving the sinful, healing the sick, bringing in
God's reign (note the present tense!)—and *he wants us in on it.*
When that happens we are ministering in the mood of Easter Sunday. *Jesus* is the resurrection and the life (John 11:25) and whoever has the Son has life (1 John 5:12). Get the emphasis on the
wrong person, on ourselves rather than Jesus, and disaster awaits
us. We find ourselves ministering in the mood of Holy Saturday.

To get the emphasis right it is helpful to develop a resistance to
approaching ministry as what Eugene Peterson once called "shopkeeping" (in *Working the Angles*). With "shopkeeping," with run-

ning the church and its programs, the emphasis shifts to us and our development of pragmatic skills for ministry. This invariably involves a shift away from attending to what Jesus is doing and what it means for us in the Spirit to share in that ministry. This is a shift away from theology (in its proper meaning as faithful thinking and speaking about God) to technique.

Let me illustrate what I intend by the last sentence and offer my contrarian perspective. (What follows may be a bit harsh, but I am trying to make a sharp point.) Pittsburgh Presbytery (of the Presbyterian Church [U.S.A.]), of which I am a member, recently gave every commissioner a copy of *Unbinding the Gospel: Real Life Evangelism* by Martha Grace Reese. I am sure it is a fine book and we should learn from it. We have been given similar books over the years. Why, I wonder, are we never given free theology books—books that have stood the test of time and been found worthy for building up the body of Christ in knowledge of God—for example, Athanasius's *On the Incarnation*, Barth's *Dogmatics in Outline* or Bonhoeffer's *Christ the Center?*

Without a clear, central theological understanding of the present ministry of Jesus and our participation in it, all the rest is just "shopkeeping." Without doubt, ecclesiastical "shopkeeping" is a good, indeed, a necessary skill to learn; for the lack of it our ministries will suffer from various functional incompetencies, and that is clergy malpractice. But there is a deeper malpractice to avoid: failing to be a participant by the Spirit in Jesus' continuing ministry. At bottom, in the deep place of Spirit power and gospel, faith and ministry are not defined by ministry management, no matter its virtue, but by the continuing ministry of the living Jesus. In fact, when ministry processes, techniques and programs have central stage, we are in very serious trouble indeed, for the reason that the living, acting Jesus has been displaced by our acting in his stead. The vicarious humanity of Christ Jesus has been replaced by the vicarious humanity of the minister! In this case we will likely find ourselves defending our ministry as "incarnational." In spite of incarnation having already happened, we often feel the need to take responsibility to make it happen once again in terms of ourselves.

The move from ministry in the mood of Holy Saturday to ministry in the mood of Easter Sunday and Ascension Thursday means reclaiming the central perspective on Jesus as an active Lord and making sure that he and not we are at the center of things. The radical hermeneutical question, not so much to be put to texts but to people's lives and situations as they confront us, is this: What are you up to, Lord, and what does it mean for me to get in on it?

The central perspective on ministry in the mood of Easter Sunday and Ascension Thursday is knowledge of an active Lord. There are two aspects to this: (1) we know of the resurrection because of the resurrected Jesus who has ascended and now sends the Holy Spirit through whom he bears witness to himself; but (2) not bearing witness only, for by the same Holy Spirit he joins us to himself to share in his continuing life and therefore in his resurrected ministry. He is the active Lord who encounters us. He is the Lord who brings us into union with himself to be about his work.

FROM PREPARATION TO ENCOUNTER

Our reflections on resurrection faith and ministry begin with the ministry of Jesus. Jesus, of course, had spent time preparing the disciples for the new reality brought into being with his death and resurrection. At a midpoint in his ministry Jesus began the education of the disciples into the deepest mystery of his ministry. "Then he began to teach them that the Son of Man must undergo great suffering, and be rejected by the elders, the chief priests, and the scribes, and be killed, and after three days rise again" (Mark 8:31). This, evidently, was a difficult lesson to learn and was followed soon after by a second. "The Son of Man is to be betrayed into human hands, and they will kill him, and three days after being killed, he will rise again" (Mark 9:31). Again, the disciples did not understand what the teaching meant. Going up to Jerusalem, a third time Jesus told his disciples this special teaching, telling them what was going to happen to him.

> See, we are going up to Jerusalem, and the Son of Man will be handed over to the chief priests and the scribes, and they will condemn him to death; then they will hand him over to the Gentiles; they will mock him, and spit upon him, and flog him, and kill him; and after three days he will rise again. (Mark 10:33-34)

After the Last Supper, on the Mount of Olives, Jesus once more told his disciples that "after I am raised up, I will go before you to Galilee" (Mark 14:28).

The shorter ending of Mark in some of the most ancient manuscripts seems to sum up the situation that remained. After the instruction from the young man dressed in white robes sitting in the empty tomb, the women "fled from the tomb, for terror and amazement had seized them; and they said nothing to anyone, for they were afraid" (Mark 16:8).

With the resurrection appearances something utterly new broke into history. Announced beforehand, the resurrection appearances make it possible to know the reality of the living Jesus in a wholly new way. The disciples testified that they were encountered by the resurrected Jesus. The New Testament has no interest in inquiring into the possibility of this encounter in a prior way by asking if such a thing as a resurrection can happen.

Neither is the New Testament interested in asking an epistemological question: How do we know that the encounters are true accounts? The encounters are given. Jesus, risen and alive, was known. The encounters with the risen Jesus changed these people, and through this Jesus changed the world.

There were many who were personally encountered by the resurrected Jesus during the forty days before his ascension. In our reflections on the resurrection appearances in Luke 24 (see pp. 29-31), we saw that the two disciples on the Emmaus Road came to believe that they had been encountered by Jesus himself. And that meeting was soon followed by another in Jerusalem as Jesus presented himself to the eleven and their companions. The disciples knew that Jesus was alive because by his initiative, not theirs, he had personally encountered them. This convictional experience has its sole ground in the self-witness of the risen Lord. This has tremendous implications for our understanding of faith.

REVELATION AS ENCOUNTER MEANS FAITH IS AN I-THOU EXPERIENCE

Jesus' teaching prepared the disciples for faith, but that teaching by itself was not sufficient. Faith is not limited to "head knowledge," to "knowing about" God. In the same way, theology is not limited to book learning in order to pass the theology test. Theology is a real knowing of God, a firsthand knowing of God, not a secondhand knowing by way of what others have said about God. Faith as theological knowing has at its center a living relationship with a living Lord. More than education is needed for faith to become dynamic and transformative. What is needed is encounter with Jesus.

Let us think about this in terms of getting to know someone. I can be told about the person I want to know. I can read about that person in the newspaper or in a book. I can see the person on television. This is knowledge to some extent, but I cannot really say that I know the person in any meaningful sense. An altogether different level of knowledge arises, however, when I am introduced to that person and begin to establish a personal relationship. Then that person and I have staked some kind of claim on each other's lives. We are changed by this knowledge. On a human level, this is knowledge through personal encounter. In the language of Martin Buber, it is "I-Thou" knowledge as opposed to "I-It" knowledge.

Something similar is intended for our knowledge of God. This is what we find, for example, at Matthew 11:27, one of the great christological verses in the New Testament. "All things have been handed over to me by my Father; and no one knows the Son except the Father, and no one knows the Father except the Son and anyone to whom the Son chooses to reveal him." This verse takes us some way toward understanding revelation as encounter, giving us an I-Thou kind of knowledge. The content of revelation is the mutual knowing of the Father and the Son, in the unity of the Holy Spirit, as the church later interpreted it. The content of revelation is a relationship: the Son knows the Father; the Father knows the Son. This knowing is not knowing about but knowing in terms of the communion of love that we call the holy Trinity. Jesus does not reveal something about God; Jesus reveals God. That is to say, revelation is not data about God seen from the outside, as it were, but sharing in the Son's knowledge of the Father, so that in Christ we know God from the inside, from within the Father-Son relationship. Jesus reveals God in terms of the consubstantial and personal relations of the Godhead, and he does so as God, from within the mutual relations of knowing and loving. To know God, according to Jesus, is to know the personal relations between the Father and the Son, in the unity of the Holy Spirit. Clearly, this is not knowledge in the sense of knowing about God; rather, it is knowledge of God that knows God from the inside, in terms of relations within God. It is to know God as person; it is to know God personally.

One more point needs to be made, and it is a breathtaking point at that: according to Matthew 11:27, revelation is making known the internal relations within God *by letting us share in them!* This is a real knowing because Jesus reveals what is his alone to share, his being as God and his communion with the Father. Clearly this is not given as something over and against us as a kind of neutral objectivity; it is given personally and relationally as, by the Holy Spirit, Jesus binds us to himself to share in what is uniquely his, his communion with the Father. We are, as it were, enfolded into the communion of love which is the holy Trinity. For this reason, theology is our talk concerning God on the ground of faith, which arises from being encountered by the living Lord who enfolds us into the Father-Son relationship. It is a form of knowing that arises from believing experience from the inside, from within the experience of being encountered by the living Jesus who unites us to himself and allows us to share in his own communion with the Father, in the unity of the Holy Spirit. That is why in this chapter it is necessary to deal with both the Lord who encounters us *and* our union with him. The two points belong together. This is the nature of revelation, and as such it is both experiential and actual.

Because of the nature of revelation as personal encounter, it is clear that this is not a process we control. Jesus encounters us in the freedom of his love. We cannot manipulate this. It is not ours to direct. Neither can we make it fit into our prior categories of meaning. Reason, rather, is converted. Understanding revelation as encounter means for us a renewing of our minds, putting on of the mind of Christ—in other words, a conversion of mind, *metanoia*—as we try to understand the life and ministry of the resurrected Jesus on his own terms.

Interestingly, this is what we find at the end of the account of the risen Lord encountering the disciples in Luke. At Luke 24:45-47 we read that Jesus "opened their minds to understand the scriptures, and he said to them, 'Thus it is written, that the Messiah is to suffer and to rise from the dead on the third day, and that repentance and forgiveness of sins is to be proclaimed.'" The natural mind cannot grasp this. Our minds must be opened by Jesus in order to understand what his death and resurrection mean (compare this with a parallel Old Testament remark about needing God to dig out holes in our heads at Psalm 40:6 [see text note]). We might well say that this calls for a baptism of mind that leads to a new mind or a change of mind: *meta-noia* (*meta* = after, with; *noeō* = to perceive or to think).

A BIBLICAL CASE STUDY: THE CONVERSION OF SAUL

One place to begin to unpack some of this complex theology is the famous Damascus Road experience of Saul/Paul in Acts 9:5 where we read of him being encountered by the risen Jesus, and who, when he was knocked to the ground and questioned, asked of him, "Who are you, Lord?" Arguably this is the central christological question, just as it contains the central Christian confession. Everything in theology that is Christian follows that form, flowing from the force of the who question, first directed to a living Lord who encountered Saul/Paul on his own terms, and who questioned him to the core of his being. The christological question contains the confession of faith: Who are you, *Lord?* Paul did not ask, "What is going on here?" "How did you do that?" "Why did I have this experience?" He did not respond, "Explain to me

what just happened." The force of the who question and the nam-
ing of the addressee as "Lord" are indicative of Paul's awareness of
being encountered person to person, as it were, by an unassailable
authority who questioned him to the very core of his being. In this
encounter Paul discovered that an absolute and unconditional
claim had been staked upon his life and destiny. So much so was
this the case that Saul, as a sign of his new identity, changed his
name to Paul.

Paul's knowledge of Jesus was based on his experience of being
encountered by the ascended and glorified Lord. This encounter
was later fleshed out and confirmed by the Spirit-sustained life of
fellowship with Jesus the Christ which followed, and that Paul
shared with his communities through his preaching, teaching
and writing. For Paul, faith does not consist in an aspiring after
God, but faith is knowledge of the risen and living Lord Jesus
Christ by way of a real relationship that takes one into the very
life of God himself. In union with Jesus the Christ, Paul did not
just know about God, Paul knew God in a hitherto unimagined
and personal way. Paul's knowing of Jesus became the fulcrum on
which everything in his life now turned. He was made a new person. His experience of being encountered by the living Lord
brought Paul into communion with him, and through this, with
the Father, in the power of the Spirit. Faith, for Paul, was knowledge of and relationship with the glorified Lord, who had encountered him on the road to Damascus. For Paul, Christian
faith, and the knowledge of God that is entailed, is both experiential and actual. The reality of being encountered by Jesus demands such a statement.

Paul's experience was multileveled. It was physical—he fell to
the ground and was blinded. It was theological—he knew immediately he was being dealt with by God. And it was utterly trans-

formative—henceforth this was the hinge on which his life turned. It is difficult to know why one would begin to ask a christological, let alone a theological, question in the first place were one not first addressed by Jesus in some way. Further, Paul's experience did not rest with knowledge and faith. The Damascus Road experience was also the basis for his apostolic commission. Encountered by Jesus, Paul now shared in Jesus' resurrected ministry. *Encounter and vocation belonged together.* This is a point of cardinal importance. The resurrection of Jesus' ministry meant both faith and a job to do. This consequence is also borne out as we know from the first disciples, from the accounts by Matthew and John, when the risen Lord did not just encounter them but in doing so also commissioned them for ministry. What this involves will be something to explore more fully later in the book.

Clearly, then, when Paul was encountered by the Lord Jesus, he was not confronted by a neutral datum of experience that he could take or leave alone. His christological inquiries were put within the framework of faith, that is, in relationship with Jesus, through whom he knew the Father. Confronted by the risen Jesus, he had before him the Lord toward whom he responded, not with quizzical nosiness or detached prying, but on his knees, with wonder, gratitude and joy as he was swept into sharing in the resurrected ministry of Jesus Christ.

FOURTH STEP: LEARNING HOW THE LORD WORKS

Through the Holy Spirit Jesus continues to encounter people, both to convert them and to draw them into his continuing ministry in the life of the world. As we move from ministry in the mood of Holy Saturday to ministry in the mood of Easter Sunday, the next step to be added to the three already noted in chapter one is the development of a specific spiritual apperception. In other words, we learn to look for and expect the hand of the Lord.

I think we learn this first of all in personal terms. We learn to notice how the Lord has dealt with us. We learn to recognize his hand at work in our lives. In the freedom of his love and through the power and agency of the Holy Spirit, I have faith because Jesus encountered me—as a lost, restless nineteen-year-old dropout; as a rookie minister who did not know how to pray; as a middle-aged man with a serious cancer diagnosis. I have faith because Jesus encountered me—through people I met, music I heard and books I read. I have faith because Jesus encountered me—through my father who taught me about compassion, my wife who taught me about love and children who taught me about growing up. I have faith because Jesus encounters me—in the sermons I hear and the Communion elements I receive, with the friends I laugh with and in the darker, quieter corners of my life where I edge toward accepting mortality and weakness. I have faith because Jesus encounters me—through theological study and debate, through my engagement with students, and even in the process of writing books. I have faith because Jesus encounters me—in my daily prayers and Bible reading.

I have faith because Jesus encounters me—through events, circumstances, people and indeed through more than I can know or imagine. Literally I may never travel on the Damascus Road, but metaphorically that is a well-worn path. As I journeyed along other roads I was and am met by Jesus mediated through the people and circumstances of my life. I cannot prove any of this in a convincing, objective manner. That does not matter because all of it is true and I have learned to recognize what's up when it happens.

For others, however, it undoubtedly is a different set of experiences. A colleague once told me that his highest spiritual experiences came through Hebrew exegesis. That was how Jesus encountered him. He learned to anticipate this encounter through the technical rigors of his academic work. Each of us is encountered as the Lord wills, and we learn to identify this.

To speak now more broadly but no less confessionally: ineffably in prayer, in thought, alone or with others, at work, at play, at our desks, on a hillside or walking along a seashore, as well as sitting in a pew or in our private prayer corner, he has met us. He has come in the Spirit in his own freedom, and all we can say is, "Thus it is so." There is no access to what we know other than its having happened: the Lord has come, and come to me. I am an encountered person. Whether our conclusions are dimly felt or sharply drawn, hesitantly confessed or triumphantly sung, we know that we have been encountered by Jesus, and as such we have been drawn into the life and ministry of God.

Of course, there is another side to all of this. Sometimes, especially when the season is dark, dangerous, wearisome, scary, lonely, despairing or at best limpid, uninspiring and routine, I choose to trust that Jesus is still encountering me, because that in part is what Jesus does. But whether I am aware of him or not, I choose to trust that in the Spirit he continues to show up within and around the edges of my life in order to draw me to himself. I choose to trust the witness of my baptism, that he has joined me to his life and ministry. I choose to trust that I am joined to the life and continuing ministry of an active Lord, even, and maybe especially, when I don't feel his presence or see his hand at work. It is during these times especially that I need the church to remind me that I remain an encountered person. The word we need to have spoken into this situation is the reminder that God acts; specifically in, through and as Jesus, and in the Spirit, God acts.

This step in the move from ministry in the mood of Holy Saturday to ministry in the mood of Easter Sunday involves being on the lookout for the hand of the Lord acting in our lives and in the lives of others. But our discernment must not be naive.

TEST THE SPIRITS

As we move from Paul to the reflection on our own experiences, we can surely say that if Jesus had no continuing ministry in the Spirit we would not be encountered by him. But is our meeting the Lord merely a private subjective experience with no external reference? No. Our sense of being encountered by Jesus must be tested against Jesus himself, as we find him attested in Scripture, and as he is known in the church. For all that Saul/Paul's experience on the Damascus Road was convicting, the apostle was required to take himself to the church, in the form of Ananias and the community in Damascus, and later to the community in Jerusalem. Private illumination can be a most doubtful platform on which to build faith and ministry—we might be deluded, we might have been presented by a spirit other than that of the Lord, but disguised as such, and so on. Test everything, we are instructed (1 Thessalonians 5:21; 1 John 4:1). Discernment is necessary. Our spiritual experiences and theological perspectives are accountable to the church's teaching and admonition (Colossians 3:16). Certainty of conviction is not a legitimate test of truth, and can in fact be very dangerous. This cautionary word, then, is in order.

A pastor told me of an alarming pastoral awareness that came to her after a number of near pastoral disasters. There was a seemingly spiritually minded person in her congregation who referred easily and with conviction of the Lord speaking to her. Sometimes these "words" involved other people. Faithfully, as she thought, she would act on these words, directing her actions and comments toward them. Invariably these "words" were heard to be harsh and judgmental, and the pastor was soon in receipt of a call insisting that the parishioner be told to back off and shut up. There was a need for discernment.

One wise friend suggested to me that sometimes we can get our sights so fixed on Jesus and on what he does for us that we forget that we too have hard work ahead, spiritual work and theological work. Grace may be free, but it is not cheap, for God or for us, as Dietrich Bonhoeffer used to remind us. So how is this testing the spirits to be done? How do we *critically* discern the hand of the Lord, in our own lives and, as pastors, in the lives of others? Scripture and tradition offer a familiar pattern against which to test our discernment.

First, we must consider the test of Scripture. In the Spirit, Jesus encounters us, bringing us to faith and commissioning us for ministry. He does this because he is a living Lord. But he remains the same Lord, not now some other Lord. He acts today as he acted two thousand years ago, with the same ministry of reconciliation. So we expect congruence between the Lord to whom the pages of Scripture bear witness and the Lord who encounters in personal experiences. The spiritual life that arises from being encountered by Jesus drives us again and again back to the Bible as we seek to answer Saul/Paul's question: Who are you, Lord? And reading the Bible brings us to an ever deeper sense of the presence of the Lord. I think of this in terms of a hermeneutical spiral that never ends, so that in an open-ended way, and always on the move, we bring our experience of encounter to Scripture, and Scripture in turn opens out our experience to new understanding. The spiritual life is not in the head or the heart, it is in the head and the heart, and in such a way that they are open to one another.

Second, we must consider the test of tradition. The church contains a wealth of theological, pastoral and spiritual wisdom, and it is wise to draw on that wisdom often. Our benefit is great indeed when we draw on the saints and doctors of the church, seeking their guidance, looking to learn from their reflections. Of course many will represent traditions other than our own, and we will be challenged by them to a more catholic perspective on the work of the Lord. But the payoff is immense as they force us to go deeper and travel wider. Reading them not only changes the perception of our personal lives in Christ; reading them will change pastoral practice as well.

In chapter one I already mentioned the five great pastoral teachers of the church. Many, many more should be added to the list: Gregory of Nyssa, Augustine, Anselm, the great Reformers Luther and Calvin, the Puritans, maybe in North America especially Jonathan Edwards, the Wesleys, the enduring Roman Catholic guides Teresa of Ávila and John of the Cross, and contemporaries like Thomas Merton, Karl Barth, Evelyn Underhill and Friedrich von Hügel. This list is merely suggestive. Dig around. New translations of classical texts abound today. It is a good time for digging. Becoming friends with the tested guides and doctors of the church is a bulwark against spiritual and theological foolishness.

FIFTH STEP: PUTTING ASCENSION DAY BACK IN PLACE

We are encountered by a living, reigning and acting Lord. Everything in Christian faith and ministry flows from this glorious affirmation. Ascension Day is parallel to and the corollary of Incarnation Day—Christmas. And as we use a spatial metaphor to describe Christmas—"love came down at Christmas"—likewise we use a spatial metaphor to describe the return of the Lord to the Father from whence he continues, through the Holy Spirit, his resurrected ministry: ascension. Without incarnation the Word would not have become flesh, and Jesus would not have existed;

without ascension our humanity would not have entered into communion with the Father, and Jesus would have no continuing ministry. With the incarnation, God made his "home" in our human place; with the ascension, Jesus, the human one, has made his "home" in God's place, from whence in the Spirit he continues to exercise his mission from the Father. With the incarnation, the ministry of Jesus on earth began; with the ascension, the ministry of Jesus from heaven began, the same Lord and the same ministry, yet different in manner, because it is now in the agency and power of the Holy Spirit. Descent and ascent run parallel to one another, completing the loop, as it were, of our Lord's life and ministry. The first means Jesus' ministry on earth, in his flesh as we know it. The second means Jesus' ministry from heaven in his flesh, now as a spiritual body and life-giving spirit.

I drive this teaching hard in class with my students. It is truly wonderful to see the scales fall from their eyes, to see the theological light come on, when they begin to grasp the significance of the ascension of Jesus. They realize that without the ministry of the ascended Lord even a resurrected Jesus slips away into meaninglessness, for there is no content to a risen Jesus without a present ministry. Everything for them in theology and ministry gets cast in a new frame of reference. Jesus becomes alive in a new and specific way, because he has a ministry to do. Christology moves from the past tense into the present tense. The old patterns of guilt-inducing thought and ministry based on a "past-tensed" moral influence Christology are gratefully and quickly discarded. They are repented of, we might say. The extent to which our ministries are wholly derivative, having their sole basis in Jesus' continuing ministry, becomes the ground for a new understanding of empowerment. Enthusiasm and energy take over the classroom.

And more: in the context of the ministry of the ascended Lord

I find the students' sense of Christian life and ministry are quickened with anticipation. The new theological imagination rooted in
Ascension Day theology and experience whets their pastoral
imaginations. Power is unleashed. The intrinsic connections between the continuing ministry of Jesus through the Holy Spirit
and the ministries of the church stimulate an eagerness for the
tasks ahead.

A further practical step, now a liturgical step, then, in the move
from ministry in the mood of Holy Saturday to ministry in the
mood of Easter Sunday and Ascension Thursday is to reclaim Ascension Day. Reclaim it as a special day of worship with its own
particular content and meaning—that is, don't just bump it to the
following Sunday to give that service an ascension tweak, but
claim it for itself, as its own day. We do that happily enough for
Christmas Day. Further, would not the reclaiming of Ascension
Day also put Christmas Day into a fresh context, perhaps going
some way toward its rescue from the horrendous sentimentality
and crass commercialism that now surround it? Undoubtedly it
will take some planning and education and overcoming of resistance, but the recovery of Ascension Day as a holy day in its own
right means the affirmation of the continuing life and ministry of
the resurrected Jesus. I dare to suggest that the recovery of Ascension Day as a major Christian festival—why not with Ascension
Day parties and Ascension Day gift giving—could spark profound
renewal in the life of a congregation, as it could in the ministry of
a pastor. The reason should now be familiar: Jesus is a living,
reigning and acting Lord.

COMMUNION WITH THE LIVING LORD
Communion with the living Lord: this is the heart of the matter as
far as Christian faith and ministry are concerned. I am referring

to what is sometimes known as the doctrine of our union with Christ. It has been beautifully defined by John Calvin in this way:

> That joining together of Head and members, that indwelling of Christ in our hearts—in short, that mystical union—are accorded by us the highest degree of importance, so that Christ having been made ours, makes us sharers with him in the gifts with which he has been endowed . . . [b]ecause we put on Christ and are engrafted into his body—in short, because he deigns to make us one with him. (*Institutes* 3.11.10)

The doctrine of union with Christ is unfamiliar for many people, yet it is central to Christian faith and ministry. It refers to the work of the Holy Spirit (Calvin calls it the "bond" of the Holy Spirit) by which we share or participate in the resurrected life of Jesus. This is the staggering claim that lies at the heart of the Christian experience. Everything in faith and ministry flows from this, from sharing in the joy and hope of the Easter Lord. This is the ground on which we build our theology, for by the Spirit who brings us into union with the resurrected Jesus, we share in our Lord's knowledge of the Father. This is the ground of our worship, for by the Spirit who brings us into union with the resurrected Jesus, we share in our Lord's communion with the Father. This is the ground of our ministry, for by the Spirit who brings us into union with the resurrected Jesus, we share in our Lord's ministry given from the Father. Thus, sharing in the resurrected life of Jesus, which is by the gift of the Holy Spirit, everything for faith and ministry is cast rigorously into a trinitarian frame of reference: from the Father, through the Son and in the Holy Spirit; and to the Father, through the Son and in the Holy Spirit.

By the Spirit, Jesus encounters us. By the Spirit we are bonded
into union with the life of the resurrected Jesus. By the Spirit we
are made members of Christ. By the Spirit we share in Jesus' resurrected ministry. It is grace from beginning to end.

What we have here is a confession of faith, not an explanation
of experience. In faith we know that the resurrected Jesus through
the Holy Spirit has claimed us, laid hold on us and joined us to
himself, thus to be part of his resurrected life. This is the central
mystery of justification by faith by which we receive the benefits
of Christ. In other words, faith confesses its trust that our "life is
hidden with Christ in God" (Colossians 3:3).

This is the meaning of our baptism that marks out the central
conviction of faith. Baptism is a declaration through action that
we have died and risen with Christ. This is not a metaphor allud-
ing vaguely to something we can't otherwise grasp, neither is it
careless or meaningless talk. Life to the self has died because we
now belong to another. Our union with the resurrected Jesus, of
which our baptism is the sign, is experiential and actual. Christian faith is the confession that, in Paul's oft-repeated words, our
life is "in Christ." Faith is the awareness that we have been brought
into a personal relationship with Jesus. But this subjective awareness is grounded in truth, in the resurrected Jesus. We don't confess faith in our experience of faith; we confess faith in the one
faith experiences because he has encountered us. And that confession entails the trust that we belong to Jesus in a personal way, as
an act of his love and power. Faith knows this to be true, not in a
way that an independent, ostensibly neutral observer could come
to a similar conclusion, but in such a way that is affirmed from
within and as a testimony of Spirit.

It is not enough, however, just to say that we are encountered
by the risen Lord. The ascension means that Jesus has a continu-

ing ministry: he presents us to the Father, he intercedes for us, and he sends us the Holy Spirit to join us to his own life and mission to the glory of the Father, for the sake of the world. It is this latter point that I now want to emphasize.

The heart of mature faith and faithful ministry is communion with a living Lord. This means sharing in his life and his life's purpose. The resurrection and ascension of Jesus, and the sending of the Holy Spirit to join us to himself, are the necessary and material conditions for faith that is rightly centered and ministry that is rightly evangelical because everything is cast on to his faith and ministry.

3

WHY DO YOU LOOK FOR
THE LIVING AMONG THE DEAD?

THE GOAL THROUGHOUT IS TO MOVE from ministry in the mood of Holy Saturday to ministry in the mood of Easter Sunday and, as we now know, also in the mood of Ascension Day. What does it look like to minister in the joy and hope of the Easter Lord? Part of what we are after here involves coming to a renewed confidence in the resurrection itself. Is it really credible? Can I believe it? Is it true? Is it more than a metaphor? And most importantly: Is Jesus really alive? In this chapter we will get down to the basic data and make an initial survey of the implications, showing practical consequences for ministry as we move along.

A helpful distinction is made between the resurrection as an event, to which we have no access, and the resurrected Jesus, who gives himself to be known by us according to the witness of the apostles. That Jesus is alive is the point of the resurrection. And Jesus gives rise to another theological question: because he is raised, what must we say about him? We want a deeper knowledge of Jesus, who was resurrected, and of the ministry that was resurrected with him. The resurrection of Jesus' ministry is a chapter in

Christology. And derivatively and subsequently we will come to a deeper understanding of the faith and ministry of the church.

THE DATA: THE ACCOUNTS OF THE APPEARANCES OF THE RESURRECTED JESUS

We have been looking at appearances by the resurrected Jesus from the beginning. It is now time to pull them all together and start to see what to make of them.

All of the information is readily available in studies of the resurrection, so I will not take much space over this. Nevertheless, some data needs to be laid out in a matter of fact manner.

The data may be ordered thus: the witness of Paul, of the other apostles and of the appearances themselves, ten in number. Without exception the data is intrinsically theological in nature.

From Paul. We have looked already at Luke's version of the Damascus Road experience at Acts 9:1-9 and made some observations. Acts records two more versions of the experience, seemingly now in Paul's own words (Acts 22:6-16; 26:12-18). There are also brief references to the event at 1 Corinthians 9:1; 15:8. The repeated reference indicates both how significant the experience was in Paul's mind and how central it was for Luke and the early church. Why was this?

The most obvious answer is that the appearance of the resurrected and ascended Jesus brought Paul to Christian faith. As noted, this was revelation as encounter. The encounter generated the who question, given as the controlling question for Christology. The two first-person accounts, however, push on further than Luke's narrated account. At Acts 22:10, after the initial conversation between Jesus and Paul, Paul asks another question, "What am I to do, Lord?" In this account, once he arrived in Damascus Paul was given his vocation through Ananias: "you will be his [the

God of our ancestors] witness to all the world of what you have seen and heard." In the later account, at Acts 26:15-18, Paul received his vocation directly from Jesus himself.

> I am Jesus whom you are persecuting. But get up and stand on your feet; for I have appeared to you for this purpose, to appoint you to serve and testify to the things in which you have seen me and to those in which I will appear to you. I will rescue you from your people and from the Gentiles—to whom I am sending you to open their eyes so that they may turn from darkness to light and from the power of Satan to God, so that they may receive forgiveness of sins and a place among those who are sanctified by faith in me.

From the other apostles. The theme of bearing witness to the resurrected Jesus is confirmed by the accounts of the other apostles. Acts 1:22 expresses what is common to the texts. After the loss of Judas, the eleven apostles, led by Peter, sought to add one other to apostleship. From among the men who accompanied the apostles "during all the time that the Lord Jesus went in and out among us, . . . one of these must become a witness with us to his resurrection." Acts 2:32 tells us, "This Jesus God raised up, and of that all of us are witnesses." At Acts 3:15 we read: "you killed the Author of life, whom God raised from the dead. To this we are witnesses." In the context of judicial defense, Acts 5:31-32 has Peter state that the Jesus whom the authorities killed is now the exalted Lord who is at the right hand of God, "and we are witnesses to these things." Acts 10:40-42 says much the same, but goes on to add that the apostles were "chosen by God as witnesses, and who ate and drank with him after he rose from the dead."

The first task of the ministry of the apostolate was to witness to the resurrected Jesus. These accounts seem to me to amount to a

significant body of evidence, validated all the more by virtue of
the strong supposition that some of these people were surely personally known to those who later read Luke's second book.

From accounts of the appearances of the resurrected Jesus. Set-
ting aside the appearance to Paul, which seems to be in a separate
category since it followed the ascension of Jesus, there are ten accounts in the Gospels and 1 Corinthians of appearances of the
resurrected Jesus during the forty days between the resurrection
and the ascension. (I have not cited all of the parallel texts to avoid
an overly confusing presentation.)

1. In Matthew 28:1-10, Jesus appeared to Mary Magdalene and
   the other Mary (the mother of James?), who had just left the
   empty tomb after the conversation with the angel of the Lord.
   Luke 24:10 adds Joanna and other women to the company who
   went to the tomb.

2. Jesus appeared to the two disciples on the road to Emmaus
   (see pp. 29-31).

3. Jesus appeared to the disciples without Thomas (John
   20:19-23).

4. At John 20:24-29, Jesus appeared to the disciples, including
   Thomas.

5. Jesus showed himself to the seven disciples by the Sea of Tibe-
   rias (John 21:1-14).

6. In Matthew 28:16-17, Jesus appeared to the eleven disciples
   before his ascension.

7. In Mark 16:9, Jesus appeared to Mary Magdalene.

8. At Luke 24:34, we are told Jesus appeared to Simon (Peter).

9. At 1 Corinthians 15:7, the risen Lord appeared to James.

10. Finally, Jesus appeared to "more than five hundred brothers and sisters at one time," most of whom were still alive when Paul wrote (1 Corinthians 15:6).

Perhaps Acts 1:3 could be added to the list, where it is noted in a general way that after his suffering Jesus presented himself to the apostles by many convincing proofs, appearing to them, and speaking about the kingdom of God.

Sixth Step: Sharpening the Edge

What to say concerning the resurrected Jesus? What a question! Surely we should pause before moving on, and take a moment to digest these plain accounts concerning the central Christian truth. Most likely we have heard the Easter stories many times. Perhaps they do not surprise us much anymore. We have read them, exegeted them, preached on them. They are the tools of our trade. We have handled them so often through the years they now fit comfortably in our grasp. There is nothing much wrong with that. But perhaps, too, this is part of what remaining with the mood of Holy Saturday is about: we are not much forced to our knees with shock, in wonder, as we read the Easter accounts. For that to happen, to use an image from Karl Barth, the familiar needs to be made unfamiliar again.

Like the tides of the ocean, spiritual and theological life has ebbs and flows. Like the seasons of nature, piety has its sunny as well as its dreary, rainy days. Our theological work has its seasons of energy and growth as well as its season of lying fallow. We learn to recognize these rhythmic patterns and don't have much cause for fretting. Ups and downs are part of the process of faith: mountaintops and valleys all have their place. But when the Easter story is allowed to fade into the general mix of ministerial routine, something terribly important gets lost in the dull relief. The sharp

contours of the Easter story give Christian faith and ministry its
edge, we might say, its cutting edge. Without that cutting edge,
ministry most likely becomes dull, for us as for our parishioners.

Certainly we need Jesus to show up. Certainly we need to feel
once more the breath of the Holy Spirit upon us. I suggest too that
there are also some intentional moves that we can make to recover
and sharpen that edge. Let us focus on worship as our workbench
where we will sharpen the edge of ministry. Each Sunday has its
special place in the liturgical year, every Sunday is also properly
understood as the day of witness to the resurrection. So this is a
good day on which to implement our intention. As we prepare to
lead the people of God in worship I suggest we make it our intent
to bear witness to the central Christian truth: Jesus is alive. How
might that be done?

Let me suggest four such moves for Sunday morning that reflect a renewed commitment to speak forth resurrection faith directly. First, intentionally speak of Jesus in the present tense. Use
all the necessary theological qualifiers: in the Spirit, through the
Word preached, as the Head of the gathered body and so on. But
emphasize that Jesus is our contemporary. There is an appropriate
sense in which he is here, in the room, about his business. In the
freedom of his love and in the presence of the Holy Spirit, Jesus is
with his people *today*. Because this is the case, something very
special is afoot. We surely cannot be dull when we speak about
Jesus in the present tense.

Second, celebrate the Lord's Supper as a communion with a living Lord. Of course there is an anamnesis, a remembering. But
there is also a Real Presence when the words of institution are
read, the prayer of thanksgiving is prayed, the bread is broken and
the wine is poured. Jesus mediates himself through the Supper as
by the Spirit Jesus joins us to share in his *life*. A frequent celebra-

tion of the Supper from this perspective bears witness to the living Lord.

Third, preach in a manner appropriate to Jesus encountering people through the Spirit. When I prepare a sermon, this is my question: What does Jesus want to say to his people? Thus I try to preach believing that the whole point is that Jesus wants to encounter his people. For me at least, that perspective gives me both a sense of urgency and the perspective that I am about a work that is truly momentous. Preach anticipating that in and through the Spirit Jesus will show up, and when he does nothing is ever the same again. Preach expecting encounter.

Fourth, bless people in the indicative mood. From my perspective there is nothing iffy about a blessing. It is not a conditional situation. A blessing is a direct statement of a situation that prevails: "God blesses you, and I am here to tell you that is so." "You are blessed!" God has blessed his people. A blessing is a remarkable event, a testimony indeed that Jesus is with his people. Yet the telling of it may become so much a matter of routine that it is heard as empty words. Bless firmly, indicatively, assuredly and declaratively on behalf of the living Jesus.

RESURRECTED AS A BODY: CONTINUITIES

Consider the continuities between Jesus as he was before and as he appeared after his resurrection. At Luke 24:13-35, for example, we have the account of Jesus and the walk to Emmaus, which we looked at already. But note now his physical presence—he walked with the two companions, he talked with them, and he ate with them. Putting aside for now the mystery of the manner of Jesus' coming and going, the corporeal specificity is remarkable, although compounded in complexity by the companions' failure to recognize him.

Continuing the story, at Luke 24:36 and following, we have the account of Jesus appearing to the eleven, their companions and the two travelers who returned from Emmaus. In response to their fear and doubt, and in view of their failure to interpret rightly what was before their eyes, Jesus says, "Look at my hands and my feet; see that it is I myself. Touch me and see, for a ghost does not have flesh and bones as you see that I have" (v. 39). Then at verse 41, in a matter-of-fact manner, Jesus asks them for something to eat. In their presence he ate a piece of broiled fish. The continuity between the earthly Jesus and the resurrected Jesus in his physical nature, as well as in his identity, is clearly in view. Further, table fellowship with the disciples was such an integral part of Jesus' earthly ministry, that his postresurrection eating with them deepens the sense of continuity (cf. John 21:12).

As a third example consider the well-known story of Thomas. Thomas had not been with the disciples when Jesus first appeared to them. Told of what had happened, he responded, "Unless I see the mark of the nails in his hands, and put my finger in the mark of the nails and my hand in his side, I will not believe" (John 20:25). A week later, Jesus again appeared to the disciples, and Thomas was with them. After the greeting of peace, Jesus turned to Thomas and invited him to test the physicality of his risen body (John 20:27). The gruesome aspect aside, there is physical continuity with Jesus as he was before his resurrection.

What are we to make of this? Jesus come in the flesh established at the incarnation has not been rejected. On the contrary, it has been affirmed in an utterly remarkable and enduring way. Indeed, we have in these accounts evidence for the resurrection of the *body*, which is in some manner continuous with bodies as we conventionally know them. It also means that Jesus come in the flesh is not now replaced by something else, but that the union of his humanity and divinity (the hypostatic or personal union) continues. When this union in the body is kept firmly before us as an enduring union, there is no danger of an account of the humanity of the resurrected Jesus being that of a disembodied Jesus.

Nevertheless, as in his life, so also after his resurrection, there was a veiling as well as an unveiling of his identity. The incognito continued. Not everyone who saw and heard Jesus during his life recognized him for who he was. Likewise, returning once more to Luke 24:16, we note that, physical as Jesus' appearance was, he was not recognized by the travelers who walked with him. There was the same nonrecognition at John 21:4, when Jesus stood on the beach and was not identified by the disciples in the boat. As with his life, was there sometimes some quality to his appearances that masked identification, or was there an act of divine concealment? This too marks an element of continuity between the earthly and the resurrected Jesus. The words of Luther continue to be valid: *Deus revelatus; Deus absconditus*: God revealed; God hidden.

SEVENTH STEP: COMING TO TERMS WITH A RISEN YET HIDDEN LORD

Ministry that moves from the mood of Holy Saturday to the mood of Easter Sunday does not cease to have to deal with ambiguity. We do not suddenly burst into the clarity of light that bathes all of ministry henceforth in its undimmed glory. In his appearances the resurrected Jesus was present but not always recognized. It is appropriate to assume the incognito would be the case also today.

This is a thought that brings us down to earth with a bump. And it protects us from a superficial, bumper-sticker triumphalism: "Jesus is the answer." Indeed we believe that is the case, but the manner in which he is the answer is not always clear to our view. No doubt the ways of God always remain clothed in mystery and it is not always immediately apparent just what it means that even incognito Jesus, through the Spirit, has showed up amid our pastoral uncertainties. On the other hand, I find it comforting to hope, on the ground of the incognito in the resurrection appearance, that more is always going on, than we glean from the quick pastoral glance.

Pastors get into all kinds of situations for which there are no easy answers, no ready solutions and no immediately realizable hopes. Pastoral dead ends are common, perhaps usual. The sin we try to address may seem irredeemable. The silence we try to speak into may seem impenetrable. The emotional pain we try to soothe may seem unfathomable. The tangled mess of life we try to untangle may seem intractable. And amid it all we may not sense the gentle breeze of Spirit presence or know the divine counsel or grasp how God's resurrection victory is even remotely applicable. A wise friend put it this way to me: "Why, if Jesus is so big, so powerful, so victorious, am I so unconscious of his presence some/ much of the time? Why, when I preach and teach the Word of the Lord are the people not bursting forth with the fruits of the Spirit? If Jesus is the reigning Lord of the universe, why are even little pastoral problems so confounding?"

These questions brook no easy answers. But a statement of resurrection faith is appropriate: Jesus has promised to be present. The issue is not whether or not we see him or recognize him. The issue is to trust that in the Spirit he is present, and pray that, as and when it is right, in his grace he will reveal his presence and purpose. Ministry in the mood of Easter Sunday and Ascension Thursday bears witness to Jesus Christ, especially aware of the incognito more often than not. This is ministry that trusts sin is not irredeemable because Jesus died and rose again for sinners. It is ministry that trusts that the silence is not impenetrable because the Word became flesh, and Jesus in the flesh is raised. It is ministry that trusts that the emotional pain is not unfathomable because Jesus is the truth, and truth lives beyond the grave. It is ministry that trusts that the tangled mess of life is not intractable because Jesus is the answer, and he will not leave us desolate. We may not see how God is working his purpose out, but that God is doing so, through Jesus and in the Spirit, is the character of pastoral faith that we take with us day by day.

RESURRECTED AS A BODY: DISCONTINUITIES

There are also discontinuities between Jesus in his earthly, fleshly nature and Jesus in the fleshly nature of his resurrection appearances. Consider the suddenness of Jesus' appearance at verses Luke 24:15, 36 and the ascension at Luke 24:51. Clearly we have entered a wholly new arena of experience and discourse. Both time and space seem to have become profoundly qualified by the actions of the resurrected Jesus.

The dramatic effect of the body of the resurrected Jesus seemingly violating accepted limits of embodied possibility is heightened by John 20:19, where the text emphasizes that the door was locked. Yet Jesus came and stood among them. We need not suppose he walked through the wood of a locked door, but only that a sealed room was no barrier to his appearing. How did he do that? The New Testament shows no interest in answering such questions. The apostle is content with the statement of what happened.

Among the accounts of the appearances of the resurrected Jesus, the event of his ascension stands out as a discontinuity within the sequence. With his ascension he was seen permanently leaving his disciples. Only Jesus' appearance to Paul broke the finality of his departure.

What conclusion do we draw? Given the overall cast of mystery and inexplicability in the accounts of the appearances of the resurrected Jesus, of central importance is that which holds continuity and discontinuity together with regard to the appearances of the resurrected Jesus. It is Jesus himself who holds everything together. The consistency lies in Jesus' continuing oneness in being in both an earthly body and in a resurrected body. Here there was no metamorphosis, as in the evolution of a chrysalis into a butterfly. "Now none of the disciples dared to ask him, 'Who are you?' because they knew it was the Lord" (John 21:12). Here there is no slight of the divine hand by which Jesus just seems to have a physical body after his resurrection. His physicality is emphasized in the texts. Restricting the accounts to an explanation of a numinous experience of some sort will not do. So the account of bringing Jesus fully to theological expression, the task of Christology, will have to include what his resurrection in the *body* means for our understanding of him. We apprehend now, perhaps more deeply, Paul's "who" question at Acts 9:5, but in view of the resurrected Jesus, as he is attested in the texts and who is present to us in the Spirit, it is now front and center our question too.

A Pastoral Question

A young woman approaches a pastor at a conference. She is mobile, but the effort is hard. Sweat spots her brow, her knuckles wrap determinedly around the two sticks that aid her walking, she drags one lame foot along the ground, and there is a deep tiredness in her eyes. "Can I speak with you?"

It is a conference on Easter themes, and there has been a lot of happy talk about the resurrection of the body. Here's the question that the young woman wants answered: "When I am resurrected will it be in this body?" She is tired of her body, burdened by its painful limitations, often hopeless when she considers the long years yet to come. Continuity between her present body and her resurrected body is not heard as good news. Yet she is personal being in this body. There has to be a hope for her with this body that for now limps painfully along.

The Christian hope is for a risen body that stands in discontinuity as well as in continuity with our present bodies. The young woman's hope is for a renewed body, her body, yet whole. Jesus was recognized in his resurrected body. And Thomas's need for empirical proof was given him. Yet, even as the resurrection body of Jesus still bore the wounds, can we be bold to say that his resurrection body contains the victory over these wounds? There is a both-and—both continuity with our present bodies and discontinuity with our present bodies. This presents us with a mystery and there is an appropriate restraint that now quickly comes into play as explanation and language fade into silence. Nevertheless, the relation of discontinuity and continuity in the body of the resurrected Jesus gives us a sense of content to our hope for the future of our bodies in which personal existence as embodied existence continues in some recognizable manner.

EIGHTH STEP: BECOMING MARTYRS

There is something to be said that is so fundamental to ministry that without saying it ministry will inevitably remain stuck in the mood of Holy Saturday: the heart of ministry is bearing witness to the risen Lord.

Ministry is a theological act. What makes it theological is what makes it ministry: *God* acts. And God acts today as God has al-

ways acted: in, through and as his Word. That is to say, God acts
through the continuing ministry of Jesus, who is present to and
for us in and by the grace of the Holy Spirit. An awful lot is at stake
in saying this.

God does not act behind the back of Jesus, as if Jesus were now
redundant or incidental to the wider purposes of God. The New
Testament affirmation of the single lordship of Jesus Christ is still
in place. That is the meaning ultimately of the resurrection of Jesus. God's ministry for salvation has an irreducible christological
character.

"God acts" means that Christian faith, life and ministry are not
built on an idealized and mythic meaning system but on a personal relationship with a Lord who acts today in time and space in
his continuing ministry of grace, love and communion. Referring
to a personal relationship with the Lord Jesus is familiar language.
But thinking about a personal relationship in terms of sharing, or
better, participating, in his ministry may be a new idea. The mag-
nitude of this is overwhelming in its actuality as good news for the
work we do.

"God acts" means that the emphasis is always placed on Jesus
Christ and not on us. The focus is on Christ's promised faithfulness to be present, as God who loves, forgives and blesses us, and
not on our experiences of being loved, forgiven or blessed, important as these are in their own way. That is, the focus is on God as
the human one who offered and continues to offer to the Father
the life and ministry that is acceptable to God.

Risk the thought that God shows up as more than the posthu-
mous influence of Jesus or as the vague hovering of the Spirit.
Something much more radical than the call to skillful caring is at
work. We need to ask, Who is Jesus Christ for us today and what
is Jesus doing? (We should also ask, What will Jesus do? but that

question need not detain us for now.) That is to say, I am appealing to a Lord who, in the Spirit, is present, acting and reigning, whose name is Jesus, who is Israel's Messiah. We must understand the practice of faith and ministry in relationship with him and in terms of our sharing in what it is that he is up to.

To participate in Christ's ministry means we share in his *life*. Who he is and what he is up to defines the whole work of our ministry. Wherever Christ is, there is the ministry of the church. To say anything less would be to dismiss the resurrection and ascension of Jesus as mere metaphors. It would be to leave him dead in Joseph's tomb. *It is not our ministries that make Christ present and possible; it is the present, living Christ who makes our ministries possible.*

Our primary job is to be martyrs. Luke 24:48 tells us that we are witnesses, that is, martyrs, in the Greek *martyres,* of these things: that the Messiah had to suffer and to rise from the dead on the third day, and that repentance and forgiveness of sins is to be proclaimed in his name to all nations. A martyr is someone who bears witness—it can mean someone who bears witness unto death, so-called red martyrdom, but it need not carry that ultimate sacrifice. It does mean that Christians give over our lives to the Lord Jesus as people committed to him. In particular as ministers of the gospel our job is to bear witness to the one who is Lord.

In all that we do the central, defining task is to bear witness to Jesus Christ, to him resurrected and reigning. To be faithful martyrs, faithful witnesses, we will be constant in prayer; committed theologians, because you cannot bear witness to the Lord if you don't know him; and loving toward those whom we are called to serve. We are called to serve Jesus Christ by bearing witness to Jesus Christ, Lord, and in doing so we will rightly serve the people and build up the church. The priority is placed where it should be. Jesus Christ first.

AN APPENDIX: EVIDENCE IS A COMPLEX SUBJECT

I have put this material in an appendix to the chapter because, while it may be helpful, in the body of the text it served to break the flow.

What kind of evidence are we dealing with when we review the accounts of the appearances of the resurrected Jesus? Evidence is a complex subject. In law it is hedged around with all sorts of caveats in order to protect the people involved and to maintain the integrity of the legal process. In science evidence is tested by rigorous experimentation that is then open to verification or falsification by the wider scientific community. Theories of evidence are debated among philosophers as each discipline develops its appropriate criteria according to the subject of its investigation. The way we investigate frogs is different from the way we investigate beauty. Just because we cannot dissect beauty with a scalpel does not mean that aesthetics is not a legitimate discipline of study and discourse, with evidence to be collected according to the nature of its subject matter. Evidence is a multilayered concept with no single, universal application. The only caveat is that the manner of inquiry must be appropriate to the subject matter, and as the subject matter changes, so too the nature of evidence will change accordingly.

We have moved away from the mid-twentieth century positivist notion of meaningful evidence consisting only of hard empirical experience that can be measured. There is no reason why we should be bullied by such imperialist philosophical aggression. Who made methods of study and conclusion about reality in any one discipline normative for all the other disciplines? Why should we suppose for one minute that all knowledge is of exactly the same nature or kind? Not all knowledge is analogous to so-called empirical science. In fact, *fact* is a problem. Science is full of challenging mysteries and faith assumptions, not the least of which is faith that nature will be tomorrow as it was investigated to be today. To give just two examples of apparent mystery from quantum theory, all light particles are simultaneously waves, and a vacuum (i.e., nothing) just appears to be empty space. In fact, a vacuum is full of virtual particles of matter and their antimatter equivalents which flit in and out of existence so fast that they usually cannot be seen (*The Economist*, May 24-30, 2008). Faith, of various kinds, and mystery seem to apply across the epistemological board.

What is the nature of evidence in theology? This is a very difficult question to answer. Let us think here of a spectrum. At the one end, in theology we make reference to events in history. Theology is subject to the canons of historical evidence. Jesus lived—at the very least that is an historical statement in the ordinary meaning of the term. But historical statements are constantly debated because they are fluid, always open to new interpretations, given that the nature of the subject matter is the past. The past is only available to us in limited ways, and therefore historical knowledge is inevitably provisional. Further, what is the nature of historical evidence for a singular event, and who decides what the canons of evidence are in such a case? In theology we deal also with ancient texts, the interpretation of which will always be an ongoing task. There are no once-and-for-all settled meanings. Authorial intent is at best an educated judgment rather than a final, definitive conclusion.

Somewhere in the middle of our spectrum we must also speak about the experience of faith as relationship with God. It is not sufficient to say, "Jesus lived." In faith we must also say, "Jesus lives." There are psychological and autobiographical elements in all theological statements, because I would not be doing theology unless I affirmed "I believe." Famously, Anselm defined theology as "faith seeking understanding." That is not to say that faith or ourselves are the subject matter of theology. Its subject is God. But God is apprehended by faith. Faith is a relationship more than it is assent to doctrines. This means, as John Calvin noted at the very beginning of his *Institutes of the Christian Religion*, that knowledge of God and knowledge of ourselves are bundled together. God encounters *us*. Yet it is *God* who encounters us. We cannot bracket our theology off from our being in a personal relationship with the One whom we try to investigate. It is from within relationship with God, then, that we seek to understand more deeply in whom we believe.

At the other end of the spectrum, theologians and preachers talk of God, who most certainly is not containable within our categories of thought and speech. How then does reference work in theology? To what kind of evidence do we appeal when we speak of God, the Lord, the Almighty, Creator of heaven and earth? How do we speak of the Creator in the language of creation? And how do we check out that our language is faithful to its reference?

In theology, clearly, the topic of the nature of evidence is vast, multilayered and difficult. Allow me, then, to pull the subject in close and ask what kind of evidence we should appeal to when we talk about the resurrected Jesus. First, there is nothing other than the resurrected Jesus to which we can appeal. He is evidence for himself. There is no corresponding analogy to the resurrection. There is nothing with which we can fill in the blank in the sentence "The resurrection is like . . ." It is time to get rid of butterflies from our church banners! The analogy does not work because there is no proportion between butterflies and the resurrected Jesus.

With the appearances of the resurrected Jesus we have an ostensible historical event that is unlike any other. Students of history, like students of science, have a great deal of difficulty dealing with singularity. Yet singularity is a defining characteristic of the subject matter of theology. That does not mean we abandon concern for evidence. It does mean that theology has to understand evidence in a manner appropriate to its own subject. But there is nothing strange in saying that is the case unless it is insisted on hegemonically that the evidence appropriate to one field of study, usually empirical science, must be applicable to theology.

Second, the resurrected Jesus appeared to the disciples—we cannot go behind them or their accounts, as it were. Our knowledge of his resurrected life is tied into the disciples' experience of him. Could it have been otherwise? We can only deal with what we are given. Our inductive theological method dictates that we build from the disciples' experience to form our conclusions. Such is the continuing nature and form of the divine accommodation to our creaturely ways of knowing. We have no access otherwise. The postapostolic saint Ignatius of Antioch is reported to have said that the resurrection took place in the silence of God. Nowhere is the resurrection witnessed, but Jesus is. So we have to trust the testimony of the disciples. The real issues around discussions of biblical authority, it seems to me, are not so much about the metaphysics of the text (its theological provenance, the nature of its authority, etc.) but about our willingness to trust the honesty and accuracy of the apostles who wrote down what they saw and heard and believed (1 John 1:1-3). The canonicity of the Bible means its use in the church. This is part of what we mean when we confess that we believe in one holy catholic and *apostolic* church.

Third, and here skeptics may find their point of attack, because faith is the category of experience that is the condition for theological knowledge, we make appeal to the internal testimony of the Holy Spirit. The church has long reflected on the significance

of John 6:69 for theological method. This verse is set in John's version of the Caesarea Philippi story that we find at Mark 8:27-30
and parallels. Because of his teaching, many of the disciples had
turned away from Jesus. Jesus asked the Twelve if they also would
go away. Peter responded, "Lord, to whom can we go? You have
the words of eternal life. We have *come to believe and know* that
you are the Holy One of God" (John 6:68-69, emphasis added).
Here is the order of coming to theological knowledge: believing
then knowing. Or, to put it differently, we come to knowledge of
Jesus as Lord only from within a relationship of faith in him, and
that is the result of his encounter with us.

4

THE RESURRECTED JESUS

IT IS TIME NOW TO PULL OUR reflections on the resurrected
Jesus of Nazareth into sharp theological focus. Everything so far
has led up to this point. There is a sense in which this chapter is
the goal of the theology of the book. If we are to move successfully,
or better, to move faithfully, from faith and ministry in the mood
of Holy Saturday to share in the joy and hope of the Easter Lord, it
behooves us to take the theology of the resurrected Jesus very seriously indeed. This is the engine room of Christian faith.

A number of topics call for discussion. I will begin with brief
comment on the central place of the resurrected Jesus for Christian faith. In this I pull together some observations that were wo-
ven into the previous chapters. I follow with a discussion that is
difficult to characterize. My theme is the nature of the resurrection, but the word *nature* seems woefully inexact, though I can
think of no other word that works better. I will then move on to
reflect on the bearing of the resurrection, first, on our understanding of the person of Jesus, and second, on our understanding of
the work of Jesus. And throughout these reflections, as in previous chapters, I will interlace a number of steps that will take us

from ministry in the mood of Holy Saturday to ministry in the mood of Easter Sunday.

JESUS IS ALIVE

Jesus is alive—this surely is the central Christian affirmation. The centrality of the resurrected and ascended Jesus means that in Christian faith and ministry the emphasis is put on his *life*. And we mean what we say. Jesus is not resurrected into a Christ principle, into a worldview or into the consciousness of the church. Neither is the affirmation a metaphor, in which we believe and act *as if* he were alive, knowing all the while that it is really not literally true.

Asserting that Jesus is alive is the central perspective of the New Testament: "If Christ has not been raised, your faith is futile" (1 Corinthians 15:17). The resurrected Jesus is the sun around which faith, ministry and all theological reflection orbit. The plain affirmation that Jesus is alive is, however, a matter of the deepest mystery and theological complexity, for his life which was lived unto death is now lived unto life. This does not mean, however, that we need get lost in technical obfuscation. After all, a theology of the resurrected Jesus must be above all a theology that will preach! Indeed, it is a theology that must be preached.

New Testament faith is Easter faith, faith in the living Lord Jesus. Jesus, living, reigning and acting is the issue. For example, notice for a moment the frequent ending to the great collects of the faith: "through Jesus Christ our Lord, *who ever lives and reigns* with you and the Holy Spirit, one God, for ever and ever. Amen" (emphasis added). That is an Easter and ascension affirmation. There, at the heart of Christian prayer, we have the trinitarian and christological structure of faith.

Like looking through the conjoined double lenses of the resurrected and ascended Jesus, the Easter community of the New Testament came to understand the person and work of Jesus entirely in terms that he who was dead is now alive in a new way. He is alive, never again to die. He is alive, Lord over all time and space. He is alive, to come again to bring all things to the Father. This means that his ministry that was ended is, with his resurrection and ascension, continuing, though now through the Holy Spirit. From Pentecost onward, the community of the Lord of Easter Day and Ascension Day is empowered in the grace and freedom of the Holy Spirit. Without being gripped by these truths, there really is no Christian faith in the New Testament sense, and there is no possibility of ministry in the joy and hope of the Easter Lord.

The emphasis is placed on the One who is sitting on the throne of the universe, *Pantocrator* (Lord of the cosmos), the One who is the truth, who is the ground of all reality, the ultimately given and living One in all his staggering complexity and mystery: the resurrected and ascended Jesus.

Ninth Step: Turn Your Eyes Upon Jesus

In 375 Basil the Great of Caesarea wrote a very famous little book, *On the Holy Spirit.* Toward the end of his discussion he refers to a tradition of unwritten teaching in the early church that included facing east when praying (§66). Basil notes it in passing, but I find the notion of intentionality helpful. What way are we facing? Or to put this differently: The direction I am facing will determine what or who I am looking at. There is an old Greek tradition that suggests the eye is the window into the soul. What we see with our eyes affects our souls. The Roman monastic tradition has a cautionary warning to "guard the eyes." This is salutary counsel in a culture in which our eyes are assaulted by all manner of things to see, much of which is spiritually numbing and person degrading. Culturally, we have become a people of the eye rather than the ear.

The pervasive influence of television is proof of that. Fast-moving images dominate our lives.

Perhaps we remain stuck in the mood of Holy Saturday because we are facing in the wrong direction and so keep looking at the wrong things. If so, we need to practice a spirituality of the eye by changing direction. For example, if, narcissistically, we keep looking in a spiritual mirror, as it were, looking at ourselves, we are not only looking in the wrong direction, we are looking at the wrong thing. Likewise, if our sights are set on looking at the congregation—its programs, ministries and so on, we are looking at the wrong thing. Or, to change the figure, we might try to limit the damage to our wounded eyes by keeping them shut tight as much as possible. That could go some way to help, but it is hardly a positive measure.

To move into and to remain firmly in the mood of Easter Sunday we need to practice looking to Jesus, the pioneer and perfecter of our faith (Hebrews 12:2). "Turn your eyes upon Jesus, look full in his wonderful face," as the song puts it—that is what I am after. And even though, as Paul says, we see in a glass dimly, that is, we inadequately comprehend the living Lord, for he is so much more than our mere words about him, when we look toward him we are at least looking at the proper object of faith. For the object of faith is not faith or the congregation or even God, understood in some general sense, but Jesus, living, reigning and acting Lord. He is the focus of our attention, and to remain so we must be intentional about the direction we face. What then must we say as we look to Jesus, resurrected and ascended, and what implications arise for ministry when we do so?

SHARING IN HIS LIFE

We follow the way of Jesus by sharing in his life. The best metaphors are organic. Like a branch connected to the vine, we abide in the Lord Jesus (John 15:1-11). We are the body of Christ, growing up in every way into him who is the head (Ephesians 4:15). Through union with Christ our lives in turn obtain a certain cast of behavior, which we find in his teaching. As we are admonished in Ephesians:

> So then, putting away falsehood, let all of us speak the truth to our neighbors, for we are members of one another. Be angry but do not sin. . . . Thieves must give up stealing. . . . Let no evil talk come out of your mouths. . . . Put away from you all bitterness and wrath and anger and wrangling and slander. . . . Live in love. (Ephesians 4:25-26, 28-29, 31; 5:2)

Because Jesus has a life, objective and given, we have a faith that has relationship with Jesus at its core and as its source, and live in a manner that reflects that relationship.

Jesus, then, is not to be understood as the founder of a religion; he is the Lord who is over all religious and moral striving. It is not we who reach him by dint of pious or moral effort—that is why the hymn "We Are Climbing Jacob's Ladder" is so seriously theologically flawed; Jesus reaches us in a free act of grace and love, binds us to himself, and in the Holy Spirit is our companion along the road of faith. This is the source of joy and hope: Jesus Christ. So, the resurrected Jesus is the central confession of Christian faith, and what this means for ministry is our continuing topic of inquiry.

THE NATURE OF THE RESURRECTION: PERSONAL IDENTITY
Here we have some difficult work to do. How do we speak of an event that is both actual and singular, that is nowhere described in the New Testament and that is entirely outside of possibility

from within the orders of creation? What is the "nature" of the resurrection? At the very least we must insist that we are entering the territory of deepest mystery.

Here is one way into expressing this mystery: the resurrection of Jesus was a historical event entirely unto itself. It was an event that only happened to Jesus. He was raised according to the action of the Father upon him. As such, it was a theological event. Whatever else this means, it means at least this: Jesus, who was dead, was raised to a form of life in his body over which death no longer holds sway. Henceforth Jesus, who is still a human, has the exercise of his full divinity within the unity of the triunity of God—what a mouthful that is! Inevitably words fail us as we try to bring it to expression, but as we walk around it, so to speak, pondering its mystery, some implications arise.

In the first place we return to a continuing point of emphasis, the continuity of the being of Jesus between his life on earth and his resurrected life: "Jesus Christ is the same yesterday and today and forever" (Hebrews 13:8). The gospel turns on this continuity. And ultimately it alone is the basis for hope. Jesus who lived is Jesus who lives. Were it otherwise, Jesus himself would have no future because he would still be dead, while some other entity would stand in his place. Were it otherwise, there would be no future in him for us, for life after death. The personal union established at the incarnation with his birth, the hypostatic union, in which he is both wholly God and wholly human, one person in two natures, continues in his resurrected life. Because Jesus was raised, who he was is who he is. Within the discontinuity of death and resurrection there is a continuity of personal and human being, though beyond the limit of death.

Personal identity is a most difficult topic to master. Who am I? Who, amid the changes of body and experience, remains still the same person? Let me illustrate the remarkable nature of personal identity through time with a brief, though inadequate, anecdote. My wife and I had the joy of a substantial Lilly Foundation sabbatical grant for clergy that allowed us to spend nearly three months in the United Kingdom in the late summer and early fall of 2007. We were able to visit some university friends we had not seen in thirty-five years, and we picked up the conversation just where it seemed we left off so long ago. But the crowning experience in this regard happened while we were wandering around my home city of Edinburgh during late August and quite unexpectedly bumped into four friends from those days. They were chatting and as I approached, one turned and said, "Hello Andrew, nice to see you"—all very matter-of-fact. It was an experience of personal continuity amid long-term change. Remarkable!

Although my experience hardly does any justice as an attempt to illustrate the theological nature of Jesus' continuing personal identity through his death and resurrection, perhaps it helps us to establish some hold on the notion. With respect to the "nature" of the resurrection, then, the first point is that Jesus of Nazareth was raised from death. In his resurrected and ascended nature (obscure as the meaning of the word *nature* is) he is none other than the son of Mary and the friend of Peter. In his resurrected and ascended life, Jesus is still Jesus.

TENTH STEP: AN EXPERIMENT IN WORSHIP

At this point I find it helpful to note again that it is important to speak of Jesus rather than of Christ or God. Speaking of Jesus keeps the continuity of personal identity clearly in focus, and this prevents us from sliding abstract theological references into our thinking. In the same manner, it opens up to view a dynamic and Christian understanding of God as Trinity. We can see this especially with regard to the language we use in leading worship.

Let me suggest an exercise that will keep our theological references on point and help us move from ministry in the mood of Holy Saturday to ministry in the mood of Easter Sunday. Review your Sunday service for *God* language, from the call to worship to the benediction, excluding nothing, and making sure to include the sermon. Everywhere you come across a reference to God or Christ, insert a trinitarian form of words and reflect whether that brings the focus more sharply onto Jesus and more dynamically onto the work of the holy Trinity. For example: "Let us worship God" could be expressed as "Let us worship God the Father, through Jesus the Son, in the power of the Holy Spirit." It is a bit clunky, but there is a dynamic movement expressed that reflects the Christian understanding of worship. In the prayers, who is addressed and how? The form here might be: "O God, our Father . . . through Jesus our Lord." We are very particular about praying in the name of Jesus, for he only is our mediator with the Father. Even in the announcements the precision is helpful: "Let me review how our congregation this week will be sharing in Jesus' continuing ministry in the blessing of the Spirit." In this way we help the people to be more precise in their liturgical reference, and at every point the continuing ministry of Jesus, as the living mediator of our worship and of our ministries, is made explicit.

THE NATURE OF THE RESURRECTION: SPACE

The second point I want to emphasize is no less difficult to grasp, namely, the theological problem of the empty tomb. I put this question to a class at the seminary where I teach: If a biblical archaeologist found the bones of Jesus, and somehow they were verifiably his, what would that do to your faith? Interestingly, a number of students found no problem with it.

Christianity, in my view, must accept the risk of empirical examination. That is to say, there is an inescapable experiential aspect to Christian claims concerning Jesus, both while on earth and concerning his resurrection. The tomb was empty because Jesus was raised bodily. Being raised, there were no bones left to find. Thus, the empty tomb is, as it were, a theological statement that is an empirical corollary to the resurrection. If his bones were found, a different conclusion would have to be drawn. That is the risk that Easter faith must take. But, in a sense, that is the point: the dead Jesus was physically raised! He is not a phantom, a ghost or a disembodied soul disconnected from his body. Creedal Christians confess faith in the resurrection of the body.

The empty tomb remains then an empirical component of resurrection faith. This, however, is easier to assert than to understand. It entails for Jesus a wholly new and singularly embodied life to which we can apply no general categories of explanation. While we have no access to the metaphysics of the resurrection, for the manner of its having happened remains God's secret, the consequence is before us: with his appearances Jesus exhibits a new way or mode of embodied human and divine personhood. The reality I am trying to speak of is the resurrected Jesus, at least in his appearances, who was at once ineffable and yet actual in his body. Paul elusively refers to the resurrected life as being a spiritual body in contrast to a physical body, but still a body, and still human in some real sense of abiding embodied personal identity.

What does this imply? The embodied, resurrected Jesus was not limited by the constraints of space *as we experience it*. Space is very difficult to define. Philosophers of science define space as that which is measured by a ruler, and therefore has extension. Theologically speaking it is space in need of redemption because, as inextricably part of creation, space as we experience it is limited by the horizon of death. In spite of the vastness of interstellar space, it remains closed space, space that is not opened out to transcendence. Jesus said, "Heaven and earth will pass away, but my words will not pass away" (Matthew 24:35). If being a body means taking up space, having mass, being measurable—and the resurrected and ascended Jesus has mass, the "space" occupied by the resurrected and ascended Jesus must be a new kind of space, a space that is congruent with his new life, space that will not pass away. It must be space that is appropriate to Jesus' resurrected, ascended and embodied life.

To be clear: I am not saying that Jesus was spaceless, for that would be to deny his continuing life in the body. In the Scots Confession (1560), John Knox of Edinburgh referred to "the selfsame body" (chap. 11) which was born, did rise again and ascended into heaven. Neither am I saying that the embodied Jesus is in every space—the theological term is *ubiquity*, and it led to terrible muddles around the understanding of the nature of the bread and the wine at the time of the Reformation. I am saying that the resurrection and ascension of Jesus involved the redemption of space. Henceforth we must think of space christologically, that is, in terms of Jesus Christ, rather than, as at his incarnation, of Jesus Christ in terms of fallen space. Perhaps we must think of eternal space, space allowing entities with measurable mass, but space opened up for new life, and not passing away. The Bible speaks of this as a new heaven and a new earth.

THE NATURE OF THE RESURRECTION: HISTORY

Reflection on the nature of the resurrection invites a consideration of the nature of history. Just as the resurrection means that space is interpreted christologically, history too has to be rethought in the light of the resurrected and ascended Jesus.

Again the philosophers of science are helpful. They tell us that time is measured by the ticking of a clock. In other words, time, as the measured interval between events, creates our sense of history. But history thought of only as "pastness" on a continuum with all other past events is no longer an adequate category for understanding the historicity of the resurrected and ascended Jesus. Certainly there was an ordinary historical aspect to the appearances of the resurrected Lord that in some manner fits into conventional historical study. There are ancient texts describing the Easter appearances that can be analyzed according to the canons of historical inquiry. And those who saw the Lord no doubt could say (to invent a context), "we saw the Lord, and on that day too we ate fish for dinner." The resurrection appearances occurred amid the regular scheme of things along with other events that make up the stuff of history.

But the subject matter itself, the resurrected and ascended Jesus, has no corresponding historical analogue. There is nothing over and against the resurrected and ascended Jesus by which he can be plotted. To say that the resurrection is historical but remains singularly unlike any other historical event is in some sense to evacuate the resurrection of historical meaning, at least in an ordinary sense of the concept. History, like space, also stands under the eschatological qualification demanded by the resurrected and ascended Jesus.

The matter is complicated further when theologians, in an attempt to reach for some kind of explanation, speak of the resurrected Jesus as the *eschatos*, as the one who, from the end of history, reaches back redemptively into the middle of history (*prolepsis*). In such a scheme, the resurrection is not a historical event in the conventional meaning of history, but is a kind of transhistorical event occurring within history, ultimately giving history its goal and thereby its meaning. Meaning in history, so it is argued, comes from the end of history, and that meaning is personal, relational and redemptive, whose name is Jesus.

What are we to make of this? At least this: at one level the resurrection is to be understood in terms of history, that is, in terms of the conventional and rigorous canons of historical study. But because conventional historical study is understood in terms of a closed continuum of cause and effect within the measured interval between events, this understanding of history must be broken open at some point in the inquiry in order to begin to consider the resurrected and ascended Jesus as a singular historical event. The canons of study must be reversed, from understanding Jesus in terms of history to understanding history in terms of the resurrected Jesus. With the resurrected Jesus, history is opened out beyond all thought of a closed historical continuum to a new hitherto undisclosed and unavailable future that is now disclosed and available. The end of history, whose name is Jesus, has broken into the midst of history: this is the assurance of the redemption of history. The dead end of history as "pastness" is not the last word in the script of our lives.

A PERSONAL REFLECTION

In order to apprehend something of the nature of the resurrection and ascension of Jesus without reductionism, without capitulating to the limited categories of conventional explanations of space and history, no matter how clever they might be, we obviously need a transformation of our categories of thought. I am tempted to say that in theology we must become "Einsteinian." As in physics, when in the development of general relativity Albert Einstein boldly broke out of the static categories of Isaac Newton's absolute time and space, so also in theology, as we are compelled by the staggering mystery of the resurrection and the ascension, we must allow all of our thinking, and especially here our thinking about space and history, to be relativized by its subject. This is the *metanoia*, the new thinking, which the theology of the resurrection demands of us (see Romans 12:2). The old, conventional categories of thought cannot hold the new wine of resurrected life.

The attempt to illustrate these thoughts is challenging. But they remain "up in the air" unless they pertain to real life. One of my favorite books is *Space, Time, and Resurrection*, written some years ago by my revered teacher Thomas F. Torrance. I want to adapt an insight from that book for purposes of illustration by way of a personal reflection.

My parents are both dead. As is customary in Scotland, they were cremated and their ashes scattered. In the light of Jesus risen and ascended, how do I understand my hope for my parents in terms of space and history? I need hardly say that this is no idle speculation, for even in their death I love my parents still very much, indeed.

I think of it this way: my parents are dead. In terms of chronological time, there are no qualifications to that reality. For them, time stopped when they died. Neither do they occupy place any more. Physically they are nowhere. The closed continuum of history and space demands these conclusions. Neither clock nor ruler can measure them any more. How then does the Christian hope, in view of the previous discussions, translate into personal terms? I choose to think that in God's time or God's history, which is history transformed from the dead pastness of the past, and in God's place, which is space opened up in Jesus Christ (I think of it as embodiedness in Christ), my parents are raised in Jesus Christ. As such they enjoy the presence of God and are celebrating at the eternal banquet. They are the church triumphant.

Thus I have to think differentially, holding two thoughts together at once that on the level of ordinary experience makes no sense, for I am saying my parents are both dead and alive. Yet on another level, of a theological level, that antinomy is resolved, and the statement makes clear sense, because in union with Jesus Christ my parents share in his resurrected and ascended life. If for this life only we have hope, we are bound to be forever disappointed. But in Christ Jesus, the resurrected and ascended Lord, history as dead pastness and space as a closed container limited by death are redeemed. History is redeemed for a new, God-given future, and space is redeemed for God-given openness for resurrected, embodied life. Thus there is a new history and a new embodiedness in Christ for my parents, for me and for you!

JESUS FROM THE PERSPECTIVE OF HIS RESURRECTION

Periodically I teach a required course in Christology as part of the theology rotation required of the students at Pittsburgh Theological Seminary. It is one course among many that I have taught through the years. But there is a sense surely in which a course on Christology is like no other. If the students get their thinking about Jesus wrong, they get everything else wrong as a consequence. Students and teacher alike stand under a huge responsibility. Like the hub of a great wheel, Christology is the center from which everything else in Christian faith, life and ministry flows. The study of Jesus Christ is the central theological task of the church. The study of Jesus Christ is also the center of the practical life of the church, for we do all things "in Christ"—Tryphaena and Tryphosa "worked hard in the Lord" (Romans 16:12); Christians are to know and be persuaded (Romans 14:14), be strong (Ephesians 6:10), speak boldly (Ephesians 6:20), trust (Philippians 2:24), hope (Philippians 2:19), rejoice (Philippians 3:1), stand fast (1

Thessalonians 3:8) and die (1 Corinthians 15:18) in the Lord. Everything—indeed, everything—in ministry is "in Christ." It is of central *practical* concern, then, to consider Jesus from the perspective of his resurrection.

JESUS' RESURRECTION DISCLOSED HIS FULL IDENTITY

Jesus is God with us and the human being with God as a living atonement, a full communion with the Father, in an eternal personal union (the hypostatic union). Let me break this down step by step.

Jesus is God with us. The resurrection tells us who was born of Mary. Apart from the resurrection the concept of the incarnation has no meaning. The resurrection of Jesus means that all along he was God with us in the flesh of his humanity. Had Jesus died, and with his death the story ended, there would be no argument that he was just a man, human like the rest of us, with no redemptive significance. The concepts of incarnation and atonement would be entirely evacuated of meaning and truth.

Sometimes we run across the argument that Jesus became the Christ at his resurrection. With the resurrection the Father validated him, as it were. My view is that this perspective is not radical enough. To say that Jesus *became* the Christ is to say also that prior to his becoming such he was not God. It means that God did not come among us, as the baby of Bethlehem, as the man of Nazareth, as the teacher in Galilee and as the crucified man of Calvary. The gospel *is* the proclamation that from Jesus' conception by the Holy Spirit and continuously throughout his life and in his death, he was God. His resurrection is not, then, the affirmation that he is now the Christ, but that he was always the Christ, precisely in and through his humanity unto death.

The message of the New Testament is that when we look into

the face of Jesus as he is attested for us in Scripture, we behold the glory and the person of God. As the man Jesus, God has entered into the deadly dramas of sinful humanity to bend us back in himself into communion with the Father. The resurrection tells us with whom we are dealing when we look to Jesus: we are dealing with God.

Jesus is also the human responding to God. This is the other side of the incarnation, and it is more often than not neglected with catastrophic consequences. It is the upward movement, as it were, as the human before God that corresponds to the more familiar notion of incarnation as the downward movement in which God comes to us as the man Jesus. As the incarnate Lord he is also, in the flesh of his humanity, the true human who offers to the Father the life of faith and obedience, trust and worship, service and love. All that the Father desires and that is wholly acceptable as a living sacrifice, worthy of God, is given by him. In the unity of his person, Jesus is God turned toward us, and Jesus is a man on behalf of all people turned toward God. In these regards the New Testament calls him the apostolic high priest of our confession (see Hebrews 3:1).

The resurrection of Jesus is the testimony that his humanity on our behalf is the Father's joy to receive. Here we have the great evangelical doctrine of the vicarious humanity of Jesus, in which in all regards he stands in for us before God, and which through the resurrection the Father vindicates as the acceptable point, or better, the acceptable person of access to the throne of grace. Jesus said, "I am the gate. Whoever enters by me will be saved" (John 10:9). Jesus said, "I am the way, and the truth, and the life. No one comes to the Father except through me" (John 14:6). The resurrection of Jesus is the vindication of this central evangelical truth: we come to the Father through Jesus Christ our Lord. That is why all our prayers and worship and ministry are offered "through Jesus Christ our Lord," as we saw earlier. I am reminded here of Fanny Crosby's great hymn which has as part of its refrain, "Oh, come to the Father, through Jesus the Son / And give Him the glory, great things He has done." The contrary position, that Jesus was not raised, has a devastating effect because we can hardly have access to the Father through the moral influence of a dead teacher.

I said a couple of paragraphs ago that the neglect of Jesus' human response to the Father has catastrophic consequences. The reason is that a failure to give appropriate attention to the vicarious humanity of Jesus means that everything, the whole of the Christian faith, life and ministry are now cast back on us to do. At the last moment, it turns out, we are dependent on *our* faith, *our* worship, *our* obedience and so on, rather than on Jesus' response for us. While our responses of course have their valid place, they are not the axis on which the gospel turns. Rather, Jesus is the axis on which the gospel turns. The resurrection of Jesus is the assurance that Jesus not only stood in for us while he lived, but that he stands in for us still, today and tomorrow and forever, offering us—who we are and what we do—in himself to the Father. Our lives, our worship and our ministries, as well as our prayers, are given to the Father "through Jesus Christ our Lord."

ELEVENTH STEP: AN INVITATION TO TRUST

The resurrection is the vindication that what Jesus offers the Father on our behalf is the Father's delight to receive. Our whole life and ministry are already gathered up in him and by him, and given to the Father. Chosen in Christ, we, lowly and inadequate as we feel much of the time, are "holy and blameless before [God] in love" (Ephesians 1:4)—even our often muddled ministries.

Here then is an invitation to trust. Trust cannot be compelled, only invited. The step envisioned here as we move from ministry in the mood of Holy Saturday to ministry in the mood of Easter Sunday is at once very simple, yet with huge implications: trust that we and our ministries are accepted by God. Why are we accepted? Embedded within the theology of the vicarious humanity of Christ—his humanity for us—is the invitation to trust that what Jesus did and does for us is adequate and worthy as he takes all that we are and do, and in his own name gives us to the Father.

To help myself with this, on the occasion when I feel down, and my sense of incompetence threatens to engulf me, I envision this glorious evangelical teaching of the Lord Jesus holding me up before the Father. The theology invites a visual representation. I picture myself being lifted up by Jesus and given to the Father, and I see the Father's arms open wide to receive me for his Son's sake. I invite you to trust that in the Spirit Jesus lifts you up to the waiting Father, who receives you, and your ministry, for his Son's sake.

Jesus' resurrection disclosed that he is the future for humankind. Jesus' life on earth was lived within the limits that we experience for our own lives. Certainly, for his own reasons, he appeared miraculously to violate some of these limits on occasion—he walked on water, he calmed storms, he turned water into wine, he had ability to foresee aspects of the future and so on. But he lived his life unto death. This was the real limit, one that was not breached. He was born through his mother's birth canal, and he died when his heart stopped beating. In the deepest and deadliest sense the Lord assumed our human life within the constraints of birth and death.

But there is no future for that human life in Jesus up to and through his death. No matter the profundity of his teaching and the wonder of his miracles, no matter the multitextured dimensions to his active and passive obedience to the Father, no matter the sublime nature of his interior life as God with us, all that ended with his death. Jesus died. The terribleness of Good Friday is the acknowledgment of this stark fact. He was really dead, or, as the creed puts it, he was "dead and buried." All of which is to say that with Jesus' resurrection the hitherto inviolable limit imposed by death—death as final and deadly—was now violated. What was not possible as an event within the created order as we know it in fact happened.

With his embodied resurrection and in union with him, his future becomes our future as his life becomes our life. It is in this sense of opening out human being to life, to a new future beyond the limit of death, that Jesus is the second Adam. He could not fully become so until his resurrection. That life which is his by action of the Father in raising him from death becomes ours by adoption, which is the consequence of union with him. This is what it means that he is Head of the race: through union with Christ, by which action of the Holy Spirit we are bonded to the living Jesus, his future becomes our future. And just as Jesus, following his resurrection, no longer lives as a human being unto death, for his humanity is now lived unto life, we, in him, are clothed with the humanity of his embodied resurrection life. In his resurrected human life, in union with him, this human life becomes the future for our human life.

When we ask, then, who Jesus is in the light of his resurrection, we are compelled to answer that he, as the true and living human, is the future for humankind. With his resurrection the fundamental structure of human being has been ineradicably altered from life unto death to life unto life through union with him. The last phrase is critical, however, and I have used it as often as I could in this brief discussion. That has been necessary. The resurrected Jesus is the future for humankind, and outside of union with him, outside of an organic connectedness to him, outside of being "in Christ"—to use Paul's descriptor, there is no future in life for anyone. The future for human life is ontologically vested in the life of the resurrected Jesus. Or as the Heidelberg Catechism puts it, "in life and death we belong to Jesus Christ."

TWELFTH STEP: THEOLOGICAL RESISTANCE TO EVIL

Untold millions of people live and die miserable lives. The problem of evil—natural evil, when nature unleashes tremendous power for destruction, and moral evil, the evil we visit upon ourselves and on one another—seems to be theologically insoluble. We all know the list—cancer, hurricanes, war, betrayal, hunger—which also seems to be practically insoluble. Moral improvement escapes most of us. Nature remains violent and deadly. If nothing else will, evil will cement us into the mood of Holy Saturday. Easter Sunday looks like a pipe dream. Our feeling of being trapped by evil is surely the devil's delight!

Against the seeming victory of evil, resurrection faith in the mood of Easter Sunday offers a life of theological resistance. We know that our resistance does not win the victory, but it bears witness to the One who does. Easter faith insists that evil does not have the last word because the first word and the last word, the *Alpha* and the *Omega*, is Jesus. Faith cannot prove this in worldly terms. But faith does not need to prove it because faith confesses and lives it by trusting in Jesus. Faith confesses and lives in terms of a new future in Jesus.

That Easter faith is the opposite of resignation and despair we are expected to say. What is not so easy is the maturity of faith that really believes and trusts that Jesus is the victory over the things that make for violence, meaninglessness and death, and that leads us to lives that make this faith concrete in action.

I have no easy prescription or program, and want to resist offering an empty piety. Nevertheless, my sense is that this maturity is gained by the discipline of abiding in Jesus (cf. John 15:1-11) rather than in the things of the world. This is a life choice, a life orientation. It means life has a specific focus, for everything else is brought into perspective in terms of accepting the Lord's claim on my life. I do not find this easy, however. The world is much with us, compelling us to think and live on its terms, and much of the time we are happy to do so, seeing no harm in it. The seduction I suspect comes in the form of thinking we can live as Christians who are at home in the world, in this culture, even in this church. In many respects we do not want to be converted by the renewing of our minds, our politics, even our theology. And we cannot live as angels, becoming disembodied, otherworldly and acultural beings. So abiding in Jesus means we have to place ourselves into a situation of real tension. I cannot give up my Scottishness for Jesus. The issue is rather how to live my Scottishness in such a manner that what increasingly shapes my living is Jesus, even though I speak of him with a Scottish accent. My invitation to live in theological resistance to evil is an invitation into tension.

Theological resistance takes the form, then, of struggle, by which in our thinking and praying and hoping and living we focus on Jesus, having him fill in more and more of the space, as it were. It involves learning a counterscript to the script society and culture teaches, and learning it deeply and transformationally. We do this in order that our perspectives and values and actions are expressions of Jesus' truth rather than expressions of the wisdom of the society and culture we live in. If Jesus is not shaping our living, something else is.

What faith confesses, then, the living of our lives intends. The theological resistance to evil is a life of active commitment to life on Jesus' terms. We live here and now in terms of that which our hope has learned to expect at the end. This is done through our political and economic decisions, as through the way we treat one another. It is not my intention to fill in the program; each of us must do that in our own voice. I do insist, however, that the Christian living in the mood of Easter Sunday must seek in all things to bear witness to the truth that Jesus lives, and that Jesus living and reigning is the criterion of political, economic and ethical truth, not self-interest, national or personal. Abiding in Jesus as a form of theological resistance to evil—and this can be quite awkward at times—expresses itself in social ethics as in personal virtue, in public life as in private life. Abiding in Jesus means going public with the truth that is in us as we bear witness in our lives to the confession we hold on to.

JESUS' RESURRECTION MEANS THAT THE PROCLAIMER BECOMES THE ONE PROCLAIMED

"Jesus came to Galilee, proclaiming the good news of God, and saying, 'The time is fulfilled, and the kingdom of God has come near; repent, and believe in the good news' " (Mark 1:14-15). This is the basic message of Jesus. He was the proclaimer of the advent of God's reign. And this he did in act as well as word, healing the sick, releasing the demonized, blessing the children, guiding the lost, teaching the confused. Not everyone who encountered him recognized who he was. And many, having some sense of what he claimed for his mission, rejected him because of that claim.

With the resurrection of Jesus, the proclaimer became the one proclaimed. For with his resurrection it was seen by the eyes of faith that the reign of God had drawn near *in and as him*. One verse may stand in for many in summing up the apostolic preaching: "There is salvation in no one else, for there is no other name under heaven given among mortals by which we must be saved" (Acts 4:12). When we ask then who Jesus is in the light of his resurrection, we are compelled to answer that "Jesus Christ is Lord, / to the glory of God the Father" (Philippians 2:11).

There is little need to labor the point here. I will only point out that when we confess that Jesus Christ is Lord, the reference is to him whose earthly ministry is now apprehended in its fullness when he is viewed from the perspective of his resurrection. Everything else follows—the authority of his teaching and the efficacy of his life of obedience to and trust in God unto his death on the cross. But the center of it all is him. The famous statement of the Lutheran Reformer Philipp Melanchthon that "to know Christ is to know his benefits" is true enough, but let the emphasis remain on the Lord Jesus. That is why the question of Saul/Paul at Acts 9:5 is so critical for Christology: "Who are you, Lord?" It keeps us focused on Jesus.

Thirteenth Step: Declaratory and Convictional Preaching

I do not think it is hyperbole to say that the intent to preach every sermon in the mood of Easter Sunday will profoundly affect both the way we preach and what we preach. In the light of the resurrection of Jesus the central task of Christian preaching is to proclaim that Jesus is Lord because Jesus lives. This proclamation makes a sermon a sermon. Religious talk, moralizing talk, even "Jesus talk" outside the framework of his resurrection and lordship is just talk. Ministry in the mood of Easter Sunday is preaching in the conviction that Jesus lives, and Jesus lives as Lord staking an ultimate claim on everyone. This preaching is declaratory and convictional, for it announces a person who reigns over all, and therefore all things are brought into proper perspective in terms of him. It announces a living way for all people. It announces truth as person in the face of all other competing claims to ultimate allegiance. It announces life where before there was death.

How could such preaching ever be dull or without effect in people's lives. Nothing is put outside the sweep of Jesus' living lordship. When a preacher catches a vision for this, surely the homiletical task is quickened. Sunday morning acquires an urgency it may not have had before. An inevitable passion rises up in the preacher's breast to push aside lassitude. Worship that might have tended toward superficiality is replaced by seriously minded proclamation. Time for intentional sermon study is eagerly set aside. The pastor's life of prayer gains a new, *dunamis*-driven intensity. In sum, ministry is transformed into the mood of Easter Sunday by resurrection preaching.

Resurrection and the Redemptive Work of Christ

From the earliest days and most assuredly after the resurrection, Christians knew Jesus as Savior—that is, as more than teacher or leader or founder, and as more than a religious genius. So rich was this faith that Jesus was Yahweh, Lord, so astonishing was their perception of this act of God for salvation, so real was this confession, inevitably it was the heart of the liturgy. In the institution narrative at 1 Corinthians 11:23-25, the connection is plainly made:

> The Lord Jesus on the night when he was betrayed took a loaf of bread, and when he had given thanks, he broke it and said, "This is my body that is for you. Do this in remembrance of me." In the same way he took the cup also, after

supper, saying, "This cup is the new covenant in my blood [which is poured out for many for the forgiveness of sins, adds Matthew 26:28]. Do this, as often as you drink it, in remembrance of me."

The central relation between the death of Jesus and salvation was an experienced reality, celebrated weekly, in the Supper.

A great number of biblical texts establish the relation between salvation and the death of Jesus. The Son of Man gave his life a ransom for many (Matthew 20:28). Jesus himself said that he would lay down his life for the sheep (John 10:15). God put Christ Jesus forward as a sacrifice of atonement by his blood (Romans 3:25). Christ was handed over to death for our sins (Romans 4:25). God was pleased to reconcile to himself all things my making peace through the blood of Christ shed on the cross (Colossians 1:20). These verses, and many more may be cited, teach clearly that Jesus died in the place of sinners for our salvation.

But there is more still to say. For Jesus as the resurrected Lord was known as a living atonement, a living reconciliation, between the Father and us. We are born anew to a living hope (1 Peter 1:3). Christ was raised for our justification (Romans 4:25). Buried with Christ at baptism we share in his resurrection that we might walk in newness of life (Romans 6:4). The fellowship of Christ's death and the knowledge of Christ and the power of his resurrection are held together at Philippians 3:10. These texts suggest there is another dimension to the atonement. On the one hand, as we saw, a proper case is made that the atonement was complete with his death. Our sins are forgiven through the death of Jesus. On the other hand, there remains still a continuing mediating reconciliation through his life at the right hand of the Father. In this way, who he continues to be unfolds into what he continues to do. With his resurrection his atoning ministry continues.

At the risk of using very clumsy language, Jesus does who he is. Jesus saves. Jesus saves as the person he was and is and ever will be. The verbs used here are very important: he saved, he saves, and he will save. When we think of the work of redemption only in the past tense, and the prevailing tendency in theology is to cast it in the past tense, the focus most likely will remain on his death. As such, the atonement is more often than not given an entirely penal and legal frame of reference. But when we cast it also in the present tense, as we must do surely in the light of the resurrection and ascension of Jesus, and with this of his continuing ministry, then a much fuller picture of the atonement comes into focus. Now we see the work of redemption as the work of his *life on earth, his death and his resurrected life*. Atonement then has past, continuing and future dimensions. Such a view includes the place of the cross interpreted in terms of Jesus dying for our sins, but extends the understanding of his saving work to include the continuing life and ministry of the resurrected Jesus.

On one level, then, with the death of Jesus, the atonement is completed. His self-offering on the cross was once and for all. In his life on earth and death Jesus bore the judgment of God on our behalf. This affirmation will always remain a central aspect of any atonement theory. On another level, the resurrected Jesus at the right hand of the Father ever lives to present himself for us directly before the Father. We are presented "holy and blameless and irreproachable" (Colossians 1:22) *in him* and *by him* to the Father. This means that the atoning mediation is also a present and continuing work.

The emphasis on the atoning mediation of the resurrected Jesus largely is missed in most atonement theories, past and present. Its importance lies in what the Lord continues to do for us. For in union with the resurrected Jesus we are brought to share in his communion or fellowship with the Father. In union with the resurrected Jesus, our humanity is now set within the Father-Son relationship in the power of the Holy Spirit. Salvation as communion with the Father means that a restored relationship with God is the defining center of what it means to be human.

Not only did the Father accept the ministry and death of the Son, but also we affirm that the Father accepts the present ministry of the Son, vindicating that he is the living, reigning and acting Lord, for Jesus ever lives to present us in himself to the Father.

A Brief Illustration

Sometimes we hurt the people we love. We act foolishly or selfishly. No love is so perfect that it fails to wound the other on occasion. And because we are loved, we are forgiven. In turn we express our sorrow. We make amends. But we know there is more still to be said, for being forgiven does not mean that the relationship is healed. There is a distance to go to move from being forgiven to restoration to fellowship. A person may forgive me for a hurt done to him or her, but that does not mean that the person wants to continue as my friend. The situation is dire when it involves a member of the family.

The analogy between our interpersonal relationships and relationship with God is at best inexact and weak. But something of similarity surely exists. Through Jesus' death on the cross, through the mystery of his atoning suffering and death, God forgives us of our sin. And through Jesus' reconciling mediation as the resurrected and ascended Lord, he brings us to the Father. Having entered a sanctuary not made with hands, Jesus appears before the Father as our advocate and intercessor, reconciles the Father's heart and prepares a way of access to the Father's throne (Hebrews

7:25; 9:11-12; see also Calvin, *Institutes* 2.16.16). Jesus restores us to fellowship with the Father, bringing the atoning reconciliation to completion.

FOURTEENTH STEP: MINISTRY AS THE PRACTICE OF THE ATONEMENT

As a young pastor thirty years ago I recall saying often to people, "God has forgiven you. You really are forgiven." I was deeply struck with the guilt that people carried around. Their sense of sinfulness and failure seemed to cripple and deplete them. Even though they were in many respects faithful Christian men and women, even though they had heard the declaration of forgiveness Sunday after Sunday, even though they felt sorrow for their sins, somewhere deep within they did not believe they were really forgiven. They felt that an angry God was out to punish them for some unforgivable sin. Thus it was I spoke words of declaration of forgiveness into their personal and often very private sense of guilt.

Looking back, I think I gave them an incomplete gospel. It was right to speak of the mercy and forgiveness of God. That remains always an evangelical indicative. And it was right to guide people in amendment of life, for it is cheap grace to pronounce forgiveness without calling for repentance and renewal. But something more was needed. They knew that something was still amiss. Perhaps they could not put it into words, but they certainly felt a distance from God, and I was largely unhelpful.

As we see from the previous discussion, the people needed to know that their relationship with God was restored. Knowledge of acquittal was only half the gospel. A further wonderful and astonishing declaration had yet to be made: "In, through and as Jesus Christ, God has not only forgiven you, God has brought you home to himself. Rest in that knowledge."

I believe that people yearn for a new relationship with God. Including, but more than, cognitive assent to doctrine, people yearn for the love of God, and to know and experience this deeply. God's love is not a vague Godly disposition, however, but is precisely the mediated reconciliation that is ours through the ministry of the resurrected and ascended Jesus who carries us to the Father's bosom. This step in ministry from the mood of Holy Saturday to the mood of Easter Sunday involves giving people the whole gospel: tell people they are forgiven *and* reconciled, acquitted *and* restored to fellowship. This step is getting us close to the center of the resurrection of ministry in this regard: ministry has made the move into the mood of Easter Sunday that proclaims the forgiveness of sins and a new life with the Father, all through the Son and in the Holy Spirit.

But giving people the whole gospel entails also attending to the demand for discipleship. This too, alas, was missing from my ministry, for I did not know that discipleship is properly the response of gratitude for a new life in God. Thus ministry is rightly cast in terms of the relationship between the indicative of restoration to fellowship with the Father and the imperatives of the obedience of discipleship. In other words it involves framing ministry in terms of the relationship between the condition for and the consequence of the gospel. Jesus is the condition for the gospel. In all regards he meets the condition: through him we are forgiven, and he brings us to the Father. In him, however, there is a consequence. Lives have a Jesus shape to them, the result undoubtedly of union with Christ but also of obedience to that Jesus shape. Just as the proclamation of forgiveness of sins calls forth repentance and amendment of life, likewise the proclamation of restoration to fellowship with the Father calls forth the commitment to discipleship by following Jesus in all things.

5

Joy and Hope in the Power of the Resurrected and Ascended Jesus

JESUS IS NOT ONLY RAISED FOR himself; he is also raised for us and for all. Jesus is not only ascended for himself; he is also ascended for us and for all. As the resurrected and ascended Lord, he is alive and reigns in power for us and for all. This is not a theological theory. His resurrection and ascension have direct consequences for our lives and ministry because he is a living and acting Lord. The ascension does not mean that he no longer has any connection with us or with all. It means that in the Holy Spirit he is present. That, at least, is what we say we believe. But I think the situation calls for some honesty.

We cannot extricate ourselves from the mood of Holy Saturday without an appropriate theological perspective and some serious spiritual effort. We are stuck in an in-between place. That image suggests something of our state of spiritual ambiguity. A big part of the problem is we may have false expectations about what living in the power of the resurrected Jesus should look and feel like.

Our Easter theology may not be congruent with the reality of sharing the life of the living Jesus.

Let me illustrate something of what I mean. In my early twenties, and as a young convert to Christian faith, one Easter Sunday in Edinburgh stands out for me. I wanted to attend an early morning service. The public transport was limited. So I bicycled about ten hilly miles from my parents' home to the congregation where I worshiped. It was a gorgeous day, sunny and warm—unusual for a Scottish spring! I recall now nothing of the service—all that remains is the memory of the weather. Easter henceforth became associated with the unexpected delight of bright sunshine. When Easter falls on a rainy or cold day, I feel oddly cheated. It can rain on Good Friday—that is appropriate, but not on Easter Sunday.

Resurrection and sunshine: that is what is in my mind. There is little to wonder about why Easter has increasingly come to be associated with the rebirth of nature and butterflies and bunnies, not forgetting the spring hats. But the truth of life is that in most places the sun does not always shine. What about Easter Day when it rains? Take that also as a metaphor. Our lives have "sunny" days when life is good, as well as "dark" days when storms threaten and we are beset by troubles. Our moods too can be sunny or dark. Am I only in the power of the resurrected Jesus when I am in a sunny mood? Surely it is during the dark days even more than on sunny days that I need the power of the resurrected Jesus.

This is what I mean when I say that we may have false expectations about Easter: it may be too associated in our minds with sunshine and all being well with the world. Of course such an upbeat perspective cannot last. The perspective is much too superficial to pass the test of life experience. It also fails to pass the test of theological adequacy. We need an Easter theology also, indeed especially, for the divorce and cancer days, when all does not feel right with our world.

FIFTEENTH STEP: MINISTRY FROM EASTER DAY TO GOOD FRIDAY

A problem arises when we do not allow Easter faith to include the dark day of Good Friday. This is demonstrated empirically in the poor attendance at Good Friday services in many of our congregations in contrast to the packed house on Easter Sunday. According to the liturgical calendar, Easter Sunday must follow Good Friday. The former without the latter makes no sense.

But I want to say something more radical than this. *Good Friday must also follow Easter Sunday.* This is where I suspect Easter faith becomes difficult for us. This is where the movement from the mood of Holy Saturday into ministry in the joy and hope of Easter Sunday is most challenging. Let me explain what I mean.

Philippians 3:10-11 sets out a framework for understanding Easter faith. Paul says that he wants to know Christ and the power of his resurrection. It is the immediate context of these words, however, that suggests their meaning. "I want to know Christ and the power of his resurrection and the sharing of his sufferings by becoming like him in his death, if somehow I may attain the resurrection from the dead." It seems there is an intentional movement here: *from* the experience of resurrection power *to* sharing in Jesus' suffering and death *to* anticipation of resurrection glory. Paul moves from Easter to Good Friday to Easter again, now as eschatological hope. This is a framework for understanding Easter faith that allows for, in fact calls for, ministry in the kind of dark, difficult and deadly places where so many people live out their lives.

The challenge of Easter faith is the call to share in the life of the living Jesus. Wherever Christ is, there is the church. Wherever Christ is, there our ministry is to be found. On Easter Day it is our joy to celebrate with him. However, his heart aches continually with loving compassion for the plight of his people. The gospel of Jesus' solidarity with the least of the brothers and sisters cannot be avoided without blasphemy against his resurrected life and its purpose. That the world still lives unto death means there is a continuing Good Friday in Christ. Insofar as through the Spirit he continues to make his home in the dark, lonely, dangerous, violent and deadly places of his creation, and with the sad, sinful, abandoned, marginalized, poor, unhappy, desperate, sick and dying people whom he loves, the parable of the judgment of the nations at Matthew 25:31-46 still applies: "just as you did it to one of the least of these who are members of my family, you did it to me" (v. 40).

As an expression of Easter faith we choose now to enter into our Lord's continuing Good Friday. In the practice of faith that moves from Easter faith to share in the Lord's continuing Good Friday, we visit in the cancer ward, in the broken home and in the funeral parlor. It takes us to the urban poor and to the rural unemployed, to the shanty towns of Africa and to the secularized coffee shops of the Western sophisticates. When we find our way to some part of this, or to some other part of Jesus' ministry in the Spirit to hurting, sinful, broken and lost brothers and sisters, we do so as ministry in the mood of Easter Sunday.

It is precisely by doing ministry in the mood of Easter Sunday that we expect to enter Good Friday again and again. But not now as the disciples felt on the first Good Friday—fearful, timid, pained and confused. We do so now knowing that the Lord is alive, that in the Spirit his ministry continues and that his victory is assured, for this continuing Good Friday, like the first Good Friday, will also be taken up and transformed into resurrection glory. We accept the call to make the continuing Good Friday our place of ministry in order to bear witness to what we confess. In view of our confession we preach and teach and heal and comfort and give hope and do our best part to relieve suffering, and especially at the grave to make our witness: "Alleluia, alleluia, alleluia, Jesus lives."

It is important to be hard-headed about this and not rush na-ively toward expectations of magic-like transformations in the situations where ministry finds us. As he did on earth, Jesus may continue to work miracles at his own choosing. But the world still groans in pain. Violence abounds. War, disease or death will claim us all eventually. Nevertheless, Paul in Philippians 3:10-11 seems to be saying precisely that ministry in the mood of Easter Sunday, ministry that takes us into difficult, perhaps seemingly intractable situations of suffering and despair, ministry that is demanding and even dangerous, is ministry in the context of a second, escha-tological Easter, announced, promised but not yet fulfilled. It is ministry in the horizon of hope. I am reminded of Winston Churchill's great speech at the outset of World War II, when he promised the people nothing but "blood, sweat and tears." We, thankfully, are offered more than that grim call to duty. For a while ministry may feel like "blood, sweat and tears," and often we may have little to show for our efforts. But unlike the people of the United Kingdom to whom Churchill spoke, we know the outcome. And more: we know that the Lord who brings about the final vic-tory is himself, by the Spirit, within us and among us, for now hidden, but always present, always doing his work of ministry so that again like Paul we confess, "I, yet not I, but the living and reigning Jesus Christ in whom we and those whom we minister among, have life and a future" (see Galatians 2:20).

Paul then looks ahead and anticipates the victory of the Lord

Jesus when all that has pitted its might against God's reign and even death itself, the last enemy, are defeated. Then Paul will know his own resurrection from death. Likewise, we labor in the context of a coming glory. We minister knowing there is an end, a limit, to evil. There is a far side to our present darkness. We see through the current situation of suffering to a coming redemption as we anticipate a new heaven and a new earth.

Ministry understood as sharing in Jesus' continuing Good Friday following his resurrection and ascension places us in the unlikely relation between joy, suffering and hope. There is joy because Jesus is alive. But suffering too is no stranger to us because in union with Christ ministry places us among the least of the brothers and sisters, there to bear witness to his love for them. And there is hope because Jesus' final victory is anticipated. Ministry in the mood of Easter Sunday, then, is ministry framed by joy .
and hope.

JOY: GOD'S VICTORY OVER SUFFERING

How can we properly feel joy in a world where there is so much terrible suffering? The newspaper headlines with their dire reports frequently disturb any sense of well-being we may have in the morning. The Scottish poet Robert Burns was onto something when he spoke of "man's inhumanity to man." Given the litany of pain and evil at every turn, should not our lives be lived in moral outrage against a God who would create and allow this? In the face of such overwhelming suffering it is easier perhaps to shut down the capacity to feel pain than to live in heightened awareness.

If joy is to be more than whistling in the dark whenever we feel alone and afraid, a phony cheeriness to keep our spirits up, then it must face these forces that seek to do us in. Faith must with confidence be able to stare them down. The faith that lives in joy and the ministry that is framed by joy must enable us to confront the darkness unto death with an alternative rendering of experience.

Biblical faith speaks of joy first of all in the context of God's victory over suffering. A pastoral verse from the Psalms sums up this perspective: "Weeping may linger for the night, / but joy comes with the morning" (Psalm 30:5). I know what it means to weep for a night, when some years ago I went through colon cancer surgery and chemotherapy. Most of us who have lived much into middle age have wept through the night. But weeping is not the final line of the story of our lives. In the Hebrew text, the word for joy (*rinnah*) means "loud crying out," "proclamation" or "singing." The best way to render the text is indeed: "Weeping may linger for the night, but JOY [shouted out loud!] comes with the morning." Biblical joy is loud and assertive, as powerful as the transitions from darkness to daybreak, from death to life, from no hope to hope, from despair to gladness, from defeat to victory.

Psalm 30 is a thanksgiving psalm that tells the story of going into trouble and coming out of trouble. We do not know the physical problem faced by the psalmist, but it is described in imagery of death and survival. In the face of death, the psalmist praises God for what amounts to a resurrection experience. At verse 4 the psalmist invites everyone else now to praise God, for such praise cannot be contained within one individual. Sing praises to God, give thanks to God, for God has overcome. The weeping in the dead of night is transformed into the joy of the new day.

This word for joy at Psalm 30:5 is used also at Psalm 126:6:

Those who go out weeping,
    bearing the seed for sowing,
shall come home with shouts of joy,
    carrying their sheaves.

Or as Knowles Shaw's (1874) song puts it:

> Going forth with weeping, sowing for the Master,
>   Tho' the loss sustained our spirit often grieves;
>   When our weeping's over, He will bid us welcome,
>   We shall come rejoicing, bringing in the sheaves."

The psalmist expresses his joy because God acted healingly in his life. Here joy is the expression of a profound inner disposition of gratitude to God that leads to loud exclamation—why not also loud, crashing cymbals, loud singing of "hallelujah." However it is expressed, it is a joy that arises in response to God's act.

SIXTEENTH STEP: INTENTIONALLY CELEBRATING JOYFULLY

Restoration to wholeness is cause for joy. Therefore ministry in the mood of Easter Sunday knows how to celebrate joyfully. It is ministry that enables people to shout out their joy over what God has done in their lives. There is nothing timid or sedate about this. It is joy expressed with exuberance.

Let me illustrate what I mean with a story. A while ago I was invited to preach at an African American Baptist congregation in Pittsburgh. I arrived early and was curious to find a congregation "warming up," getting their praise juices flowing. Choir and band and arriving congregation seemed to take about half an hour before the service started to "get up to speed." After a while five men in their twenties, dressed in white robes, came in from the side door. Deacons prepared the baptistery. One by one they came forward for a full immersion. And as each man came out of the water the organs played crashing chords, the choir sang hallelujahs, drums beat out a rhythm and some eight hundred or so congregants were on their feet cheering and clapping and singing. This was a people who understood the meaning of baptism: from death to life. There was indeed something to celebrate.

Different church and theological traditions will express themselves in diverse ways. But let there be intentionality in expressing the community's joy—over birth, over a person coming to Christ, over a vocation discovered, over marriage, over anniversaries, over lives well lived, over healing, over money raised or a building built, over retirement, over sin repented and so on—in the faith that God acts in people's lives. That God acts is never to be taken for granted but always to be received with gratitude and great joy.

Joy: God's Victory in Christ

Our principal theme, of course, is joy in the context of Jesus' resurrection. At John 16:16-24 Jesus makes the connection explicitly. Once again the disciples had trouble understanding that Jesus must die and be raised, so Jesus spells out his meaning. He tells them they will weep and mourn his death. The world will rejoice at this pain. But their pain will be turned into joy. Just as a woman in labor has pain during childbirth, once the baby is born she no longer remembers the pain because of the joy of new life. Likewise, Jesus tells his disciples, you too will have pain. But he assures them that they will see him again, and their hearts will rejoice at this, and the joy they feel will not be taken away from them. And the Father, says Jesus, will give them what they ask for, and their joy will be complete.

A specifically Christian account of joy grounds our joy in the resurrection of Jesus Christ. But in a general way too the New Testament puts the whole gospel story into the framework of joy. Luke, for example, announces that the Christian gospel of God's redemption in Jesus Christ, beginning and end, is cause for joy. The message of salvation is announced to the shepherds by the angel of the Lord: "Do not be afraid; for see—I am bringing you good news of great joy for all the people" (Luke 2:10). In the beginning there is joy, indeed, great joy, because Jesus' birth is good news. Joy is the key signature of the gospel. After the ascension, at the end of the story, Luke narrates that the disciples worshiped Jesus and went on their way back to Jerusalem, again with great joy (Luke 24:52). So at the end also there is great joy, because the Lord Jesus reigns and rules. In Matthew, joy is associated with the women's experience at the empty tomb when the angel announced the message of the risen Lord (Matthew 28:8). Joy—because Jesus overcomes sin, evil and death and is now alive forevermore.

Joy has its source in Jesus. He is our joy—who he is, what he has done and what he continues to do for us. The birth, death, resurrection and ascension of our Lord are the grounds and the occasion for the Christian's joy. Joy is the consequence of knowing Jesus and living our lives in him. Christian joy, then, is not cheeriness. It is rather a profound trust in Jesus and in what he promised he would give us. "I have said these things [about abiding in him] to you so that my joy may be in you" (John 15:11). So the Christian's joy comes from abiding, living deeply, in Jesus, and through that having a confidence in the Father's love, trusting in God's victory over death.

JESUS' JOY

At John 15:11 the Gospel refers to Jesus' joy. Jesus explains that he has said these things about abiding in him so that his joy may be in the disciples. What is Jesus' joy that is his gift to us?

For Jesus, joy surely was a profoundly personal and intimate experience that arose from his unbroken communion with the Father. This communion constituted his being as Emmanuel. Because he was God the Son, his life was lived in the mystery of the unity of the holy Trinity. Even on the cross, when he struggled mightily with his sense of abandonment and dereliction, he could still end with an affirmation of trust in who he was and what he was about: "Father, into your hands I commend my spirit" (Luke 23:46). His joy takes us into the deepest life of and relationships within the unity of the holy Trinity. It could not be otherwise. In practical terms, Jesus' joy was expressed in his keeping of his Father's commandments and his abiding in his Father's love.

At Hebrews 12:2 we travel further into the mystery of Jesus' joy, for the writer tells us that Jesus "for the sake of the joy that was set before him endured the cross." The journey to the cross certainly has religious, social and political dimensions. But its inner and deepest meaning is that it was a course he took for us and for our salvation. It was his joy that he took on the sins of the whole world as the means of redemption. It was the fulfillment of his innermost being as the Son of the Father, as Emmanuel, as God with us and of his mission from the Father, as God for us.

This does not mean that Jesus took a masochistic delight in suffering—such a view would be both ridiculous and blasphemous. Rather, in the deepest sense imaginable, Christ's joy, the fullest expression of his profound union with the Father and of the Father's love for us (see John 3:16), was his atonement for our sin, his at-one-ment with our plight and his bearing of its consequence on the cross of Calvary. Jesus' deepest joy was not found in the avoidance of his cross, as much as that was humanly desirable (Luke 22:42). In a manner that utterly transcends our sense of joy as a mere upbeat emotion or as cheerfulness, Jesus found his deepest joy in enduring the cross for what that meant in his service of God and of you and me. His joy at the end on the cross surely had to do with the completion of his life on earth as the one who in his death gave life to the whole world. The cross is not the failure and the resurrection the victory. The cross is itself the victory, and the resurrection—that is, life—is its consequence.

This joy, arising from Jesus' intimate union with the Father and the work of salvation, is the gift that he now shares with those who love him. Jesus' gift is to let us into his own relationship with his Father through our union with him. Thus Jesus prays at John 17:13 "that they [the disciples, and you and I] may have my joy made complete in themselves." How wonderful it is that Jesus' will is for us to be joyful by being filled with the joy of his salvation, sharing through union with him in his own deepest intimacy with God. For the sonship that is his by nature has now become ours by grace through adoption (Galatians 4:5).

SEVENTEENTH STEP: THE JOY OF MINISTRY

Joy, a little one-syllable word, hardly seems sturdy enough to carry the full weight of Christian fulfillment. How easily it just slips by. We would hardly think such a small word would be adequate to sum up the meaning of sharing in the life of the resurrected Jesus. Yet it is precisely accurate to say that ministry in the name of Jesus is indeed rightly characterized as ministry with joy.

Ministry with joy is the fruit of abiding in Jesus. This is another way of insisting: say your prayers, read your Bible, study theology, learn to discern the presence and agency of the Holy Spirit. Including what we must do, however, ministry with joy is also the gift of Jesus to us. And as a gift, it is to be received with gratitude, tended with care and applied with delight. Ministry with joy, then, is ministry that is purposefully attentive to the giver and the gift, and humbly mindful of the responsibility. It is ministry that trusts the Spirit presence of Jesus at every turn and knows his ministry continues into the life of every person we encounter and every situation we confront. It is ministry in the confidence that *he* continues to be the Savior and that salvation is not our work to worry about. It is ministry that has laid aside all messianic pretensions and therefore rejoices in carrying the lesser burden.

On the other hand, I meet many ministers—in my Doctor of Ministry classes, at conferences, often too through e-mail—who tell me of their weariness, sense of failure and lack of delight anymore in meeting their round of pastoral work. In the language we are using here, they have lost the joy of ministry. What is needed is not more time spent on "how to" or ministry technique books. The malaise is usually not from lack of skill but is spiritual in nature.

The malaise is certainly spiritual if a minister is not abiding in Jesus. Only by making that abiding our first responsibility will we share in his joy. The connection between abiding and joy is intrinsic to John 15:1-11. The reasons why a minister is no longer abiding in Jesus are most likely not hard to find: too busy, too busy, too busy—with all manner of church work, with every task of ministry. When this happens the sour fruits are lassitude, weariness, lack of centeredness, loss of direction, boredom and the like. I have discovered too that with this malaise a minister may take avenues to excess to try to ease the pain: affairs and too much drinking are sadly not uncommon. It is time then to take a spiritually necessary and honest "time-out." A realistic and informed assessment of spiritual life is urgently required. Not for the first or the last time, it is time to start again.

Make an honest assessment, and if needed, get help. Find someone wise in ministerial wiles, who will not let you off the hook with easy answers. Through the years I have found Gregory the Great's *Book of Pastoral Rule* (George E. Demacopoulos, 2007) to be the epitome of sage counsel and insightful admonition. (Gregory became pope in 590. Even Calvin thought him a legitimate teacher of the whole church.) Perhaps a spiritual director would be helpful. Most Roman Catholic residential communities are quite comfortable these days working with Protestant ministers who seek spiritual counsel. Ask around, find out who has been helpful for others. Take time for some spiritually attuned reading—the great teachers and saints of the church are mostly readily available today in new translations. Whatever seems appropriate, get to it before a crash happens, for then great damage can be done.

THE HOPE OF RESURRECTION FAITH

Joy cannot be separated from hope. The hope of the gospel, and the only real basis for joy, is that God in, through and as Jesus Christ has entered into the darkness of our plight unto death and brought light and life into the world. For Christian faith, to speak of hope is to speak of Jesus Christ. While the Christian's hope has to do with the Christian hoping, it has much more to do with Jesus and what our life in union with him means for our future and indeed for the future of creation. To put that differently, in thinking about hope we do not just think about hope as such, as an affective state, but about Jesus Christ who is our hope because we share in his life.

As always, then, Jesus is our subject matter. This does not mean that I place no value on hope as a subjective experience. On the contrary, hope as a human experience in the face of suffering and death is a wonderful thing. There always remains a hoper who hopes. But with Easter faith in the resurrected Jesus, hope is not its own subject.

The first topic to arise in thinking about hope is death. The Grim Reaper will wield his democratic scythe in our direction too. While the denial of death (see Ernest Becker) may well be a feature of our society, death nevertheless is both all around us and at work within us (2 Corinthians 4:12). Its terrible finality presses upon us, and there is a sense of urgency and pathos that quickens our attention, demanding a response. A theology of hope is compelled to address the issue of what happens when we die. Or to put that differently, how can we have hope when we know we will die? And we must reflect too not just on our own deaths but also on the dying and deaths of those we minister among. For a pastor, death demands our response on a very frequent basis.

In the New Testament the Christian hope in the face of death is based on the resurrection of Jesus. The classic text is 1 Peter 1:3: "By his great mercy [God] has given us a new birth into a living hope through the resurrection of Jesus Christ from the dead." Or again: "God raised the Lord and will also raise us by his power" (1 Corinthians 6:14). At John 14:19 Jesus says, "because I live, you also will live." More generically, perhaps, Acts 23:6 reads that Paul is on trial concerning hope and the resurrection of the dead. And further, "If for this life only we have hope in Christ, we are of all people most to be pitied" (1 Corinthians 15:19). The early Christians believed that the resurrection was not only a sign that Jesus was alive but a guarantee that they would live also beyond death. My first point, then, is this: Hope trusts that what happened to Jesus will happen to us.

It is interesting to note that the funeral service in some church circles is not called the Service of Christian Hope, as if now, at the last, everything is to be cast back on ourselves, our faith, our hopes and our theories of eternal life. Rather, the funeral service is called the Witness to the Resurrection. There is something profoundly instructive in this. Everything—and truly we can speak in terms of the last analysis because this is as final as anything gets to be—is cast back upon Jesus Christ, into whose future we trust ourselves and one another and ask God for the faith to rest in that. Hope does not point back to itself but away from itself to the risen, ascended Jesus Christ.

Resurrection faith believes that eternal life has been given to us in Jesus Christ. What faith believes, hope expects. Hope has the same goal as faith: because Jesus lives, we will live also in him.

EIGHTEENTH STEP: A FUNERAL IN THE MOOD OF EASTER SUNDAY

The Christian funeral is an eschatological event. In the service we primarily look forward to the work of God in raising the dead, which is promised for those who are in Christ Jesus. As such, it is surely self-evident to insist that nowhere else is ministry in the mood of Easter Sunday more appropriate than at a funeral. The focus is uncomplicated: a dead person and a living hope for that person because we trust what Jesus promised. At the funeral we can give ministry in the mood of Easter Sunday all the freedom and space we can muster to trumpet its message: Jesus is alive, and in the confidence of that confession the funeral is declarative and convictional in tone and content.

Funerals and customs around the dead are often peculiar, localized and can be very touchy matters indeed. And ministers wisely do not get too creative or idiosyncratic in their funeral leadership. Funerals mostly are conservative events. Nevertheless, customs and expectations accrue that may reflect the culture more than the faith. So the following is suggestive of what I think a funeral in the mood of Easter Sunday would entail.

Faith in Jesus our living hope can be confessed anywhere. But some places are probably more helpful than others in adding sight, sound and feel that are congruent with the Christian hope. Thus I have requested that my funeral be in the church I worship in, among the people of the congregation in our familiar place of meeting. A strong case can be made for church funerals. Why, at the last, would anyone want the final act of the church in a person's life to take place in the secular and commercial environment of a funeral home? Why would this most solemn act of faith be located otherwise than in a church?

The Christian funeral is rightly weighted by biblical texts that bear witness to Jesus' resurrection and the hope for those who are in Christ. This emphasis would also shape the preaching and the prayers. The Christian funeral is characterized by forward-looking, christologically controlled speech, not by backward-looking, eulogizing speech. That is not to say there is no appropriate place for a eulogy—it reminds us that this is the funeral of a real person, loved by those in attendance. It is to say that the funeral is the liturgical expression of eschatological faith, and that resurrected-based speech and resurrected-informed hope anticipate a future in Jesus for this person.

I also think that it is appropriate and helpful to celebrate holy Communion at a funeral, though in my Scottish Presbyterian tradition I have rarely seen it happen. The Supper is profoundly an expression of life and death interpreted in view of Easter faith. As much as it is a meal of remembrance (*anamnesis*), the Supper is also a meal of Real Presence and future hope. We recall that the Lord Jesus, on the night on which he was betrayed, took bread . . . "Do this in remembrance of me," he said. We believe too that in his Spirit he draws us up to himself that we may feed on him, the living bread. Here is comfort for those who mourn. But further, we interpret the Supper to be also an anticipation of the eschatological banquet, where the church triumphant feasts in glory with the Lord Jesus. With appropriate explanation it is appropriate to celebrate the Supper at a funeral as a visceral expression of eschatological faith.

THE HOPE OF SALVATION

The second matter to reflect on under the rubric of hope is the issue of sin and forgiveness. Calvin used to say that sin was adventitious, meaning that it was accidental and not intrinsic to who we are as human beings. As such, it was not really explainable. There remains something irresolvable about sin. Its malignant power can only really be understood in terms of what God had to do to overcome it. At its core sin is a broken relationship with God, and as such it remains a mystery.

Atonement is intrinsic to the gospel. The hope of the gospel is not only a future in Jesus Christ for those who suffer, the dying and the abandoned, but also a future in God for sinners. Every pastor knows that a major pastoral problem still is the extent to which so many people lack confidence in their salvation. People may remain unsure that their sin is really forgiven. The hope of the gospel at this point is to show that God's grace in Jesus Christ applies also to them. Or to put this in relational terms: people need to be told that the broken relationship with God, which leads us to act sinfully, has been healed.

Romans 4:25 was a favorite text of many of the Reformers: Jesus Christ our Lord "was handed over to death for our trespasses and was raised for our justification." Atonement for sin and the bestowal of a positive righteousness belong entirely to the work of Christ, culminating in the resurrection. Hope then is trust in the assurance of forgiveness that arises from the work of Jesus on our behalf.

My teacher, the late Scottish theologian Thomas F. Torrance, used to tell us of helping his little daughter to walk. Many decades later, he could still feel the touch of her hand in his hand. And when she would stumble, it was his hand that held her firm. Torrance used this image to speak of our new life in God through Jesus Christ. In Christ and through the Holy Spirit, God has reached into the lostness of our humanity to hold us firmly by the hand. Stumbling around, on the verge of toppling into the vast abyss of sin unto eternal death, Christ grasped us—"even there your hand shall lead me, / and your right hand shall hold me fast," said the psalmist (Psalm 139:10).

When we in faith, as a gift of grace, reach to hold the hand of God, it is but to discover that we are already held securely, for God's hand is upon us (Psalm 139:5). This truth is told dramatically in the Lord holding Peter's hand as he tried to walk on the water, lost faith and started to sink (Matthew 14:31). Our hope for salvation does not lie in the fact that we hold on to God's hand, as if our decision and act were the principal part of the economy of hope. Rather, our hope for salvation lies primarily in the fact that God's hand in the humanity of Jesus Christ has already reached out for, found and held fast to our hand. The radical consequence of sin forgiven and the bestowal of a positive righteousness means placing no trust in our own goodness, piety or good works, but placing our hope entirely in the grace of Jesus Christ alone.

In Easter hope we expect a future beyond death on the basis of Jesus' resurrection. Likewise, we have hope for our sinful pasts and our coming sinful futures of disobedience and faithlessness on the basis of Jesus' atonement and its acceptance by the Father in his resurrection. This is not a hope that God someday will break the vicious cycles of death, destruction and violence that characterize our living, or that we will suddenly get the message and begin to live ethically and sinlessly. It is the hope based on the knowledge that Jesus Christ already has entered into these vicious cycles, turned them from death to life and restored us to a new humanity, and that in union with him we are called day by day to live out our Easter faith in his victory.

NINETEENTH STEP: LITURGIES OF FORGIVENESS

To illustrate something of how hope in the assurance of sin forgiven might be a focus for ministry in the mood of Easter Sunday, I suggest that there is a need for liturgies of forgiveness. There are two aspects to this. The first is the need for people to hear again the declaration of God's pardon and to express their acceptance of it. The second is the need for people to declare forgiveness to one another.

In Roman Catholic, and some Anglican and Lutheran, congregations there is a rite of reconciliation in which people can express their sin in a liturgical context. This acted-out confession can be a helpful way of moving from sinfulness to acceptance of forgiveness. Protestants, of course, do not accept the need for a sacerdotal mediation—the work of a priest—but the notion of an act of reconciliation seems helpful to me.

Consider the situation of a divorcing couple who are members of the church. Put aside for now the issue of the theological legitimacy of divorce. Let us accept it as a stubborn reality: for whatever reason, Christian men and women fall out of love or act hurtfully toward one another and the relationship breaks. Given divorce, is there a way to help the couple to move forward without acrimony and bitterness?

As an exercise in pastoral imagination, consider offering a liturgy of forgiveness. Most likely it would be private or in the company of family and close friends. In the context of words of gospel grace, each would be invited to say, before God, their words of repentance. Simply put, each would confess sin. Each would be invited to say to the other their words of repentance. Simply put, each would express sorrow for past behavior. The minister would declare the mercy of God. Each would say to the other words of forgiveness.

I cannot say if such a liturgy of forgiveness would reconcile the marriage because I have never heard of one being performed. I suggest, however, that with such a liturgy of forgiveness something of the mutual hurt and anger has been expressed, heard and received. Repentance before God and one another has been spoken. In such a context the call for amendment of life has some hope for traction.

HOPE FOR TRANSFORMATION

Jesus Christ is Lord over all of life. A theology of hope, therefore, must be a theology for the transformation of the world. A hope promised by the gospel that does not seek to bear witness to the reign of God in the midst of our economic and political experience would be no hope at all. We must address not only the obvious concerns around death and sin, but also the profoundly biblical concerns for social righteousness as well. Put bluntly: Christians living faithfully should make a difference in the world. We will not establish the fullness of the reign of God, of course, but surely we can expect some movement in that direction.

Christian hope does not catapult us beyond the earth. It does not lead us to abandon life in history. Rather, hope is a way of life on earth and in history in obedience to the call to discipleship by sharing now in the Spirit-present resurrected ministry of Jesus. After all, if we claim to be in relationship with the incarnate, world-affirming, history-redeeming Lord Jesus Christ, we might well expect that that relationship would leads us to participate through the Holy Spirit in his continuing redemption of the evils under which his people live and die.

All theology is done and all faith is lived in the contexts of murder, torture, starvation and death. Hope in the living Lord draws us into his opposition to existing reality which has no truth in it, as we share in his incongruence with the status quo that defies the reign of God. Knowing the power of Jesus' resurrection we are set free for hope-expressing life in him to be critical and transformative of the processes that make for death and the loss of hope.

Christian hope does not dissolve hope into politics. But it is in obedience to Christ that Christians place themselves into situations that call out for transformations, for the hope of the gospel must also be seen as hope for the poor and the exploited, wherever they are to be found. A ministry of hope that does not take the risk of concrete engagement ultimately fails to be a ministry of hope, becoming instead a faithless sitting on the sideline for fear of contamination. Faithfulness always means the risk of involvement.

Let me give some concrete illustrations of what I have in mind. Some are more provocative than others, and each of us will have to find our own way into this kind of ministry. Many congregations are actively involved in Habitat for Humanity and similar ministries. Others take time to work with the mentally disabled or with tutoring elementary students in basic writing and reading skills. Peacemaking ministries are common, as are ministries that address hunger, homelessness, teen pregnancies, drug use and so on. Christian people are members of Amnesty International and regularly write letters on behalf of political prisoners. We do not cast off our Christian identity on Monday morning. What then does it mean to be a Christian in industry, commerce and trade union work, in education and health care? What does it mean to be a Christian in politics, in the police or the military, in the foreign service or in international aid work? What is the right relationship between Christian faith and civic responsibility?

These illustrations and questions serve to suggest the extraordinary scope of potential Christian ministries of transformation. As always the primary issue is discernment: where in the Spirit is Jesus at work in the world, and what does it mean for me to be part of his body in union with him with regard to that work?

"Grace to you and peace from him who is and who was and who is to come" (Revelation 1:4).

6

Ministry in the Power of the Resurrected Jesus

Throughout I have inserted steps that indicate how we move from ministry in the mood of Holy Saturday to ministry in the mood of Easter Sunday. These steps have been offered to suggest the way forward. They are not prescriptive in the sense of a twelve-step program. I want now to characterize ministry in the mood of Easter Sunday. To do that I have selected six biblical and creedal statements and the characteristic of ministry that arises. This list is not exhaustive but suggestive of ministry in the joy and hope of the Easter Lord. What I have to offer, as always, is Jesus, living, acting and reigning in the power of the Holy Spirit.

Ministry in the joy and hope of the Easter Lord should have a distinctive orientation. I am not trying to package Jesus into a program of ministerial or congregational renewal, however. His reality as living Lord is far too vast for that. But we may have confidence to make a vigorous affirmation of the life and ministry of the resurrected Jesus and to no longer remain stuck in the mood of Holy Saturday. In the Holy Spirit we share in the life of Jesus. And as the living one, his ministry continues. It is the actuality of his ministry that makes our ministry possible.

MINISTRY AS DOXOLOGY: PRAISE GOD FROM WHOM
ALL BLESSINGS FLOW

Doxology: "Praise God from whom all blessings flow." The basic orientation for everything in Christian faith, life and ministry is the praise of God's glory. "Do everything for the glory of God," Paul instructs us (1 Corinthians 10:31). In the familiar opening words of the Westminster Shorter Catechism: "What is the chief end of man? Man's chief end is to glorify God, and to enjoy him forever." It is our joy to give God the glory in all things. Specifically, this means placing all that we do in the context of gratitude to the Father, through Jesus the Son, in the unity of the Holy Spirit for God's victory over death, sin and the powers of evil.

The ground for giving God the glory is singularly and specifically the life and future of the resurrected Jesus. If we would live and minister doxologically we will need to hear again and again, and vigorously, the significance of the resurrection of Jesus' life and ministry. The significance of the resurrection of Jesus' life and ministry is the glory of God and our future in glory: not just forgiven, not just raised to eternal life—we are also forgiven and raised for glory, for the delight of God and for communion with God. We anticipate a new heaven and a new earth in which the whole scope of human history is gathered up by and in Jesus Christ through the will and power of God to make all things new. "Father," Jesus prayed, "I desire that those also, whom you have given me, may be with me where I am, to see my glory, which you have given me because you loved me before the foundation of the world" (John 17:24).

The boundless majesty of the glory of the great consummation is beyond our capacity to imagine. Our thinking is just too earthbound. But the New Testament gives us some words that point in the right direction. From Philippians 3:21: "[Jesus Christ] will transform the body of our humiliation that it may be conformed to the body of his glory." First Peter 5:1 refers to one who shares in the glory to be revealed. Paul at Romans 8:18 tells us that "the sufferings of this present time are not worth comparing with the glory about to be revealed to us." In other words, the New Testament refers to a state of blessedness into which believers are to enter hereafter through being brought into the likeness of Jesus Christ.

> Death has been swallowed up in victory.
>> Where, O death, is your victory?
>> Where, O death, is your sting?
>> The sting of death is sin, and the power of sin is the law.
> But thanks be to God, who gives us the victory through our Lord Jesus Christ. (1 Corinthians 15:54-57)

These words have a reference that grounds them in the reality of the living Lord Jesus and his present and future ministry on our behalf. In union with Jesus Christ, faith is opened out to the future and is characterized therefore by the mode of hope.

As our Lord is one in communion with the Father and the Spirit, so we in him share in that glory which is his. "The glory that you have given me," Jesus prayed, "I have given them, so that they may be one, as we are one" (John 17:22). This is both a present and a future reality, and is at the end what our union with Jesus Christ means. In and through that union we are eternally marked as children of our heavenly Father, to share Christ's life and love in the communion of the holy Trinity.

Ministry in this frame of reference, ministry as doxology, will be marked by confidence in God's victory and a future with God for all God's people. This is a confidence that knows that the last words in the script of the lives of the people among whom we minister are not words of defeat, despair and death. Ministry in this frame of reference knows that cancer, divorce and violence are not the final acts that determine the fate of people in our pastoral charge. The last words will be "Welcome home." The last act will be the embrace of welcome into God's "house." This we must tell our people again and again.

It is foolish not to recognize that there is something deeply counterintuitive about praising God when the script of life seems to conclude with defeat, despair and death, and when divorce, cancer and violence seem to win in the end. In view of the aching sadness, paralyzing fear and grinding hopelessness experienced by so many millions of people every day, singing praises to God seems on the surface to be morally offensive. We cry out for God to act now, and we have scant answer to our critics when not a lot changes for the better. In this context Christians must carry out ministry as doxology in the horizon of hope, for it is not yet the time of the end. Doxology without hope is empty of content and would be as pastorally insensitive as it would be theologically incompetent. So let us move now to think about ministry as doxology in the horizon of hope.

MINISTRY IN THE HORIZON OF HOPE:
AMEN, COME LORD JESUS

On the ground of a past work of God, we minister in anticipation of a future work of God—the advent of God, a final redemption in the future, a life beyond the grave and a fulfillment of history beyond death.

For faith, life is opened to a future characterized by the promise of God contained in the life and ministry of the resurrected Jesus, a promise out of the past that creates a horizon of openness for the future. This promise creates an open horizon of expectation as the faithful await the coming fulfillment with hope—we have a future shaped from beginning to end by the life and ministry of the resurrected Jesus. The loss of hope, on the other hand, is the loss of faith in both the past of Jesus' resurrection and the future of Jesus' life and ministry. The loss of hope is what happens when we turn away from the resurrected Jesus, when we believe in effect that Jesus is simply dead. Perhaps the loss of hope in this sense is now the characteristic expression of atheism today.

The ground of Christian hope lies in who was resurrected, for as truly God, Jesus our brother took our deadliness into the life of God, and in his resurrection brought new life out of that deadliness and gave it a future. The heart of the promise is often missed: resurrection is not just something that happened to Jesus but something that, through our union with Christ, will also happen to us. Sharing in his life is to share in the promise of that life and the future that it entails. Resurrection then must be thought of not just as a doctrine of faith to be believed, but also as a personal apprehension of trust in the promise of God given to us in the life of the resurrected Jesus. Hope means life lived in the horizon of expectation of our future with Jesus.

Pastorally speaking, the ground of hope that must be proclaimed and celebrated, that constitutes the ground and content of ministry, is that Jesus lives. This is the ground and truth of all Christian prayer and worship. Without it, prayer and worship become the fruitless task of religious self-actualization. This is the ground and truth of all Christian comfort. Without such hope, comfort is without strength (*com fortis* = with strength). It is a lie. A hope in a vague sense of God, a hope that is not christologically specific, a hope that turns the resurrection into a metaphor or a social experience, is a hope that will dissipate in the face of blunt, deadly reality, leaving us with hope only in our own resources. And that, unfortunately, is a well-tried recipe for despair. If Jesus Christ is not raised, not only faith but also hope and ministry are in vain.

Pastoral work is always in one way or another a ministry of hope: because Jesus lives, we too, because we share in his life, will live as well. This word of assurance, on the basis of this promise, must ever be on pastors' lips. The ultimate word, the decisive word that is ever and always announced is: Christ is risen! Life!

But yet more must be said, for we do not just live within the horizon opened up by promise and a future in him. We live also in the horizon opened up by the anticipation that Jesus will come again. Especially in mainline Protestantism today, little is said about this. Perhaps, truth be told, we are a bit embarrassed by it. But here is the issue: a promise is not much good if there is no assurance it will be fulfilled. In fact, not much good, even, is the sense of being in relationship with Jesus now if for this life only we have hope. To put this in theological terms: the resurrection of Jesus is not much good if he will not return and do for us what the Father did for him. So, cast aside any embarrassment we feel concerning the second advent. The fulfillment of the gospel resides in the affirmation of faith that the living Jesus will come again to bring all things to the Father. That, in short, means a future life in Christ Jesus for those whom he draws to himself. This we must preach with firm conviction, for otherwise, our people are left in despair.

Allow me a personal testimony. My father died two days before my first son, Brendan, was born—twenty-seven years ago this week, as I write this. He died of lung cancer. The deepest sadness of my life, and a subject still of emotional confusion, is that my father did not live to know and watch his first Purves grandson grow up. Brendan's birth was announced to my extended family in Scotland at my father's funeral. My father knew Brendan only in anticipation. Here is my understanding of the Christian hope through our union with the living Jesus who will bring us home. Jesus, Dad and I will enjoy, in some way, meeting together in the kingdom of God. For although we glimpse this fulfilled hope most surely in a mirror dimly, even so, I want to insist that there is truth here—a personal future in glory with those we love.

In summary, the point I am making is that hope that is not concrete is no hope at all. This is not mythological thinking, which is creaturely thinking projected on to God. It is firmly realist thinking, for it arises directly out of the gospel and the meaning of the affirmation "Amen, come Lord Jesus." In ministry, let us bear witness to this hope in the midst of the pastoral life of our congregations.

MINISTRY CLOTHED WITH WONDER:
AND THEY WERE AMAZED

And of course, all this is amazing. Understanding that ministry involves our sharing in the life of the resurrected Jesus, our ways of thinking about ministry must be adjusted accordingly. This calls for a true *metanoia*, a real change of mind. Categories of thought are broken open and expectations change because the center of attention has shifted from what we do to what the resurrected Lord is doing. This in fact involves a profound hermeneutical change of perspective. Perhaps it reduces us to a wondering silence, because the skill sets have to change as well, and for a while we may be more baffled than enlightened. As I have pondered this and allowed myself to be drawn into the amazement of Peter as he stood in view of the empty tomb (Luke 24:12), I have come to think that wonder is part of the essential characteristics of sharing in the ministry of the resurrected Jesus.

By way of illustration, consider Jesus' references to the faith of children, indeed, to the leadership of children in the life of faith. This suggests to me something of the importance of wonder. Wonder characterizes children's experience. They are continually astonished. Big-eyed and delighted, they inhabit their world in wonder, amazed at the colors, patterns and sounds, at the animals and the bugs, at the tastes and smells. So Jesus bids us to learn again, this time from the children, of wonder.

Perhaps we (adults) are still too much the inheritors of Enlightenment rationalism: we think too much, explain too much and know too much. The mystery at the heart of everything is masked by function and utility. We are masters of our universe, wresting all within our grasp to our own ends and supposed needs. But I have a fancy that faith should be slow. It takes time to notice what's around us, to be curious and to ponder the extraordinariness that is in everything. I have a fancy that faith should be quiet. It takes the time to listen and to accept silence as a gift to be grateful for. I have a fancy that faith should be curious. It accepts mystery as part of the nature of things and people, and as such, sees, as it were, into the heart, not only of people but of mountains and clouds, of falling leaves and newborn kittens. I have a fancy that faith should be empty. It welcomes space and challenges our addiction to stimulation. That, most likely, is why fasting is really a form of subversive prayer. Well, I am certainly in need of this sermon!

Without some of this, without slowing down, becoming quieter, allowing curiosity to arise and resisting filling our emptiness with junk, there can be no wonder, especially wonder that arises because we notice God's gracious mischief in people's lives. The wonder that arises from faith in the resurrected Jesus expects open horizons, novelty and surprise. Wonder is the correlate of faith in a living and acting Lord who, as likely as not, moves quietly, subtly and often hiddenly in people's lives. But move he does! When there is no wonder, have we not locked God out of our world? A faith without wonder has no place for the resurrected Jesus.

Thus far there has been an eschatological perspective as we have thought about ministry in the power of the resurrected Jesus. Ministry clothed with wonder begins to bring us down to earth. It affirms God's movement into every context and situation, *and expects to see the consequence*. No corner of existence is God-deprived, so ministry clothed with wonder expects miracles. Wonder at the acts of the living Lord characterizes the resurrected ministry of the church, not in a past dispensation but today. Wonder becomes a central hermeneutical perspective that allows us to see the hand of God that blesses, to hear the voice of God that comforts and admonishes, and to be aware of the presence of God that empowers. Wonder, then, is a spiritual apperception—a way of apprehending the world because the Lord lives and acts.

Characterized by wonder because we share in the resurrected ministry of Jesus, what does ministry look like? Here are some suggestions. Never leave home without anointing oil. Bless people. Expect that Jesus in his Spirit is up to something in people's lives, and oil is a symbol of that ministry. Never get into a pulpit without the expectation that Jesus wants to say something to his people, through your brain and vocal cords. Never sit at a committee meeting in church without conscious and articulated awareness that the common task is spiritual discernment of what the Lord is up to in that room. Never pick up a book on theology or exegesis or church leadership without expecting the transformation of mind, the enrichment of soul and the challenge to do ministry because the Lord lives. Practice the spiritual discipline of becoming big-eyed. Expect to be astonished, indeed, anticipate astonishment. Perhaps then ministry becomes wonderful/wonder-filled.

MINISTRY WITH BRAVERY: TAKE COURAGE; I HAVE CONQUERED THE WORLD

Ministry with bravery no doubt should be thought through on many fronts. In this section, however, my focus briefly is on preaching. The pulpit is the public place of ministry and most likely is the place where bravery or timidity will show itself. But note, the issue is not the virtue of courage or its lack in the preacher, but the preacher's conviction or otherwise concerning the life and ministry of the resurrected Jesus.

Allow me a sad story of timidity in ministry. During the late summer and early fall of 2007, my wife and I spent three months in the United Kingdom. We heard sermons in small country chapels and huge urban cathedrals, as well as in ordinary parish churches around the country. Drawing general conclusions from this sampling is a risky business. Nevertheless, one impression drawn from the preaching we heard was confirmed through many private conversations: christological timidity. Time and again preachers pulled back from the affirmation of a risen and acting Lord. There is surely a connection between ambiguity regarding Jesus as a living Lord and dreary, ineffective preaching. The church in Great Britain seemed to be on tiptoe, going about its work trying to make as little noise as possible, so that one is not even sure it is there at all. As far as we could tell, loss of Christology in theology had the effect of eliminating power from the sermon. In spite of much homiletical noise, we wondered too where our theological timidities get in the way of clear, brave proclamation of the gospel.

The daily lectionary during the period of my writing this chapter has included selections from the Acts of the Apostles. One thought especially has struck me: the preaching of the early church upset people. The lively account of the effect of Paul's preaching in Ephesus, recorded in Acts 19, is a good example. Apostolic preaching stirred things up because it was centered on Jesus, the resurrected Lord. No timidity there.

Why does preaching become weak and vapid? Perhaps, as I suggested, one reason may lie in the preacher's loss of confidence in, or even faith in, the ministry of the resurrected Jesus. Obviously, there is not a lot left to say if Jesus remains a dead moral and spiritual influence. If we are timid about faith in the resurrected Jesus, our preaching will reflect that. Preaching is evacuated of power and limited in truth. Another reason may be found in a reluctance to provoke and rather to let sleeping religious convictions lie for fear of what might happen if they were awakened. Whatever the reason, I suspect there is direct connection between preaching with power and effect, and trusting that a living and acting Jesus in the freedom of his love and in the presence of the Spirit will address his people here and now. If indeed the defining homiletical task is to bear witness to the Lord who speaks to his people, believing he is mute is massively counterproductive.

At times honest preaching will undoubtedly get us into trouble. It will upset the comfortable and comfort the upset. Proclaiming that Jesus is Lord means that other claims to divinity have no truth in them—the divinities of nation, class, power and so on. Proclaiming that Jesus is Lord means that there is salvation in no other name (Acts 4:12). This is a direct challenge both to the claims of the religions and to the broad acceptance of religious diversity that God has many names, and that there are many paths to this God. How to preach into the contexts of multiculturalism and religious pluralism with courage, truthfulness and conviction, as also with respect, sensitivity and kindness toward people of other faiths, is a huge challenge. Bravery in proclamation does not mean rashness or arrogance or demonizing other faiths or their adherents.

Preaching with bravery arises from spiritual groundedness and theological acuity. We cannot proclaim the name of Jesus faithfully without living in that name; we cannot proclaim the name of Jesus truthfully without knowing him who bears that name. Behind the public face of the preacher in the pulpit is the man or woman of faith steady at prayer and disciplined in study. Bravery in ministry is the fruit of bravery in faith, the courage to trust in the life and ministry of the resurrected Jesus, and with clarity and conviction to bear witness to what it is he wants to say to his people.

MINISTRY THAT IS CHARISMATIC:
AND HE BREATHED ON THEM

A person cannot be "in Christ" and not have the gift of the Holy Spirit. Faith: it is by the Holy Spirit that we confess Jesus come in the flesh (1 John 4:2). Ministry: it is by the Holy Spirit that we are bonded (Calvin's word) to Jesus Christ, thus to share in his life and ministry. *Charis*, grace, leads to *eucharistia*, thanksgiving, and to a life that is *charismatic*, Spirit-gifted attachment to Jesus. It is about time that the whole church reclaimed the charismatic nature of Christian faith, life and ministry.

Acts 1:8 reminds us that the gift of the Holy Spirit is the gift of power—*dunamis*—enabling disciples to be witnesses, both near and far. Ministry in the power of the resurrected Jesus, charismatic ministry, is characterized by vocation and act. Let us look at these in the light of Acts 1:8.

Vocation comes from the call of God. Vocation means being sent out by Jesus to share in a specific way in his resurrected ministry. To that end, vocation is dependent on being breathed on by Jesus, on the gift of the Holy Spirit, who does not empower us from a distance, as it were, but who joins us to himself to share in his resurrected life and ministry. Ministry is "in Christ." Vocation, then, is God-called, Spirit-empowered, Jesus-connected discipleship that has sharing in the ministry of the resurrected Jesus at its center, as its defining content. Call, sending and empowerment seem to be the basic structure of ministry, while Jesus' continuing mission from the Father is its content.

As such, vocation leads to act, to the concrete events of ministry. There is nothing "airy-fairy" about sharing in Jesus' resurrected ministry, nothing generic or vague. Vocation as act moves far beyond sympathy or well-meaning good intentions. Vocation that leads to act is the public sign of the concrete ministry of the resurrected Jesus. Just as the lordship of Jesus means nowhere and no one is excluded from his ministering presence, likewise vocation leading to act means Christians must expect to be both radically worldly and immanently specific. That is, in Christian ministry characterized as "in Christ" we are both placed in the world and made present to actual situations in a hands-on way. Vocation that leads to act is "up close and personal."

Consider Jesus' example of compassion found throughout the Gospels. The Greek word for compassion, *splagchnizomai*, means literally to have one's bowels turned over in solidarity with the suffering of another person. Moved with compassion Jesus touched the leper and healed him (Mark 1:41). Moved with compassion for the widow of Nain, Jesus touched the bier and raised her dead son (Luke 7:13). At Mark 9:22 the desperate father of the epileptic boy calls on Jesus to have compassion. When the youth went into another seizure, Jesus took him by the hand and healed him. Moved with compassion, Jesus touched the eyes of the two blind men and healed them (Matthew 20:34). At Matthew 9:36, compassion is used by the apostle to sum up Jesus' ministry.

The accounts of Jesus' healing, compassionate touch is indicative of the intimacy, actuality and immediacy of ministry as act. There is a face-to-face quality, something of presence and involvement. It is ministry by way of making connections, even of physical relationships. What is especially interesting here is that in the Gospels only Jesus is described as acting with exactly this kind of compassion. To put this theologically, only in union with Christ will we share in his compassionate touch. In union with Christ we must expect to be led vocationally to empirical situations that cry out for healing, and where the resurrected Jesus is present already, ahead of us. (For a full account see my *The Search for Compassion: Spirituality and Ministry*.)

Ministry in the power of the resurrected Jesus is more than a ministry of eschatological hope. I have tried to show here that it also involves a concrete and specific engagement in the life of the world. As we are called and empowered to share in the ministry of the resurrected Jesus, we expect to go to where he is actually involved in ministry today. Ministry that does not become concrete and specific in this regard may be judged as having missed the point.

MINISTRY SUSTAINED BY THE LORD WHO REIGNS: SITTETH AT THE RIGHT HAND OF GOD THE FATHER ALMIGHTY

In this section I put ministry in the power of the resurrected Jesus into a cosmic context. My reason for doing so is my fear that often our horizon with respect to ministry is too low, our vision is too small and our expectation is too limited. In which case, with limited perception we may fail to see beyond what is within our immediate reach and sight. We may fail to grasp that we are partners with Jesus in salvation work that is cosmic in range. I suggest that while ministry is local, as indicated in the previous section, each local act is part of a cosmic work of God's redemption that plays out on a scale that is so immense we cannot get our minds around it. We are players in heaven's symphony, but we neither write the score nor conduct the orchestra. Everything we do and say is part of a mighty work of God, for we look not just for the salvation of this world, but for a new heaven as well as a new earth. The vista within which we go about our work is nothing short of a new creation. What is equally remarkable is our vocation to play a part in the present work of the resurrected and ascended Jesus to that end.

The resurrected Jesus sits at the right hand of God the Father Almighty. It is worth pondering the immensity and purpose of this for a moment, even if the theological complexity of what it means may be quite beyond our understanding. Nothing is now outside the sweep of Jesus' resurrected and ascended life and ministry. Nothing—no caveats or qualifications apply—is beyond him. All creation now is within his saving and sustaining purview, from the dark vastness of interstellar space to the statistical probabilities postulated by quantum physics to the life of a new born baby. He is the creator and redeemer Logos, the cohering source of rationality, the ground of meaning, the personal act of truth, the human actuality of divine love. How do we bring that into the perspective of ministry?

Consider Psalm 139:7-10:

Where can I go from your spirit?
  Or where can I flee from your presence?

If I ascend to heaven, you are there;
    if I make my bed in Sheol, you are there.
If I take the wings of the morning
    and settle at the farthest limits of the sea,
even there your hand shall lead me,
    and your right hand shall hold me fast.

Or consider Paul when he asks who will condemn us. Note his answer. "It is Christ Jesus, who died, yes, who was raised, who is at the right hand of God, who indeed intercedes for us" (Romans 8:34). The range and purpose of the Lord's ministry means there is nowhere we can go to take us outside of the range and consistency of his love.

The Lord does not have a parochial, partial or uncertain reign. He is Lord of all, ruling over all space and time. He is Alpha and Omega. One thing this might mean for ministry is that it puts our efforts into perspective. The success of God's redemptive plan is not our responsibility. It is God's responsibility, indeed God's act, to inaugurate the kingdom in fullness. There is a very real sense then in which we should think about what it means to rest in the completeness and adequacy of his reign. Important as our work is, so much more important is his work. Painful as our failures surely are to all concerned, including God, they are never the last word. Ultimately, it is not up to us to exercise messianic ministry, and certainly not on a cosmic scale, so let us not even try. The kingdom is not carried on our shoulders.

Another way of saying all of this is that ministry is rightly seen within the providence of God. Jesus' reign at the right hand of the Father is a summons to have confidence in God's ordering of all things, and so, therefore, to be less anxious about our own small part in the economy of creation's salvation.

Ministry confident in the fulfillment of the promise "Behold, I make all things new" is ministry that trusts Jesus' reign and his final victory. As the resurrected and ascended Lord, all things are under his feet. All things are gathered together for his purpose. And as he rightly is the end, let me stop and simply say again what all the foregoing has tried to proclaim: Jesus lives! And in the end, glory! In the end, glory! In the end, glory! Even so, come Lord Jesus.

Author Index

Scripture Index

Acts
1:3, *69*
1:8, *148*
1:22, *67*
2:32, *67*
3:15, *67*
4:12, *107, 147*
4:18-20, *17*
5:31-32, *67*
9:1-9, *66*
9:5, *51, 76, 107*
10:40-42, *67*
22:6-16, *66*
22:10, *66*
23:6, *129*
26:12-18, *66*
26:15-18, *67*

Romans
3:25, *109*
4:25, *109, 132*
6:4, *34*
8:18, *139*
8:34, *152*
12:1, *37*
12:2, *32*
14:14, *98*
15:54-57, *139*
16:12, *98*

1 Corinthians
2:16, *37*
6:14, *129*

9:1, *66*
10:31, *138*
11:23-34, *108*
15:6, *69*
15:7, *68*
15:8, *66*
15:17, *34, 86*
15:18, *99*
15:19, *129*

2 Corinthians
4:12, *128*

Galatians
2:20, *119*
4:5, *126*

Ephesians
1:4, *101*
4:15, *89*
4:25-26, 28-29, 31, *89*
5:2, *89*
6:10, *98*
6:20, *98*

Philippians
1:20, *109*
2:11, *107*
2:19, *98*
2:24, *98*
3:1, *98*
3:10, *109*

3:10-11, *117*
3:21, *139*

Colossians
1:22, *110*
3:3, *62*
3:16, *56*

1 Thessalonians
3:8, *99*
5:21, *56*

Hebrews
3:1, *100*
7:25, *112*
9:11-12, *112*
12:2, *88, 125*
13:8, *90*

1 Peter
1:3, *34, 109, 129*
5:1, *139*

1 John
1:1-3, *83*
4:1, *56*
4:2, *148*
5:12, *44*

Revelation
1:4, *136*